SCOTNOTES
Number 25

directed by
Michael Caton-Jones

Rob Roy

David Manderson

Illustrations by Angelica Kroeger

Association for Scottish Literary Studies 2009

Published by
Association for Scottish Literary Studies
Department of Scottish Literature
7 University Gardens
University of Glasgow
Glasgow G12 8QH
www.asls.org.uk

ASLS is a registered charity no. SC006535

First published 2009

A CIP catalogue for this title
is available from the British Library

ISBN 978-0-948877-94-0

The Association for Scottish Literary Studies
acknowledges the support of the Scottish Arts Council
towards the publication of this book

Printed by Bell & Bain Ltd, Glasgow

CONTENTS

SCOTNOTES

Study guides to major Scottish writers and literary texts

Produced by the Education Committee
of the Association for Scottish Literary Studies

THE ASSOCIATION FOR SCOTTISH LITERARY STUDIES aims to promote the study, teaching and writing of Scottish literature, and to further the study of the languages of Scotland.

To these ends, the ASLS publishes works of Scottish literature; literary criticism and in-depth reviews of Scottish books in Scottish Studies Review; short articles, features and news in ScotLit; and scholarly studies of language in Scottish Language. It also publishes New Writing Scotland, an annual anthology of new poetry, drama and short fiction, in Scots, English and Gaelic. ASLS has also prepared a range of teaching materials covering Scottish language and literature for use in schools.

All the above publications are available as a single 'package', in return for an annual subscription. Enquiries should be sent to:

ASLS, Department of Scottish Literature, 7 University Gardens, University of Glasgow, Glasgow G12 8QH. Tel/fax +44 (0)141 330 5309, e-mail **office@asls.org.uk** or visit our website at **www.asls.org.uk**

EDITORS' FOREWORD

The Scotnotes booklets are a series of study guides to major Scottish writers and literary texts that are likely to be elements within literature courses. They are aimed at senior pupils in secondary schools and students in further education colleges and colleges of education. Each booklet in the series is written by a person who is not only an authority on the particular writer or text but also experienced in teaching at the relevant levels in schools or colleges. Furthermore, the editorial board, composed of members of the Education Committee of the Association for Scottish Literary Studies, considers the suitability of each booklet for the students in question.

For many years there has been a shortage of readily accessible critical notes for the general student of Scottish literature. Scotnotes has grown as a series to meet this need, and provides students with valuable aids to the understanding and appreciation of the key writers and major texts within the Scottish literary tradition.

Lorna Borrowman Smith
Ronald Renton

1. INTRODUCTION

The Real Rob Roy

The film *Rob Roy*, produced by Peter Broughan, directed by Michael Caton-Jones and starring Liam Neeson and Jessica Lange, was released in 1995. It was the latest in a long line of texts (which in this booklet means both books and films) based on the exploits of a legendary Scottish figure but also a real man, a famous Highland leader who lived in late seventeenth and early eighteenth century Scotland.

The real Rob Roy (1671–1734) – so-called because of his striking red hair (the name comes from the Gaelic *Raibeart Ruadh*, or 'Red Robert') – was a complex and controversial individual.[1] He had many followers, who were mostly members of the 'proscribed' – meaning banned or outlawed – MacGregor clan, and he was admired by many others, particularly among the common people of the Highlands, for whom he seems to have had legendary status within his own lifetime. His enemies, who included great Highland landowners and politicians in London and Edinburgh, regarded him as nothing better than a rebel and a thief. He took part in the major historical events of his day, including the Jacobite Risings of 1689 and 1715, the latter of these in support of the 'Old Pretender' (the son of James II, the last Stuart King, ousted from the British throne by William of Orange in 1689). He was present at the battles of Glenshiel and Sheriffmuir, had his clan lands seized and was declared an outlaw. He lived by practising cattle-theft and a legal system of protection known as 'blackmail', where for a fee his followers would 'protect' a landowner's cattle (meaning they would not steal the beasts themselves). At different times in his life he was hunted across Scotland and had to hide from government soldiers and the private armies of the great landowners. He made many daring escapes from capture and many bold counter-attacks on his pursuers.[2] He was eventually imprisoned, but escaped. He took part in the disputes between the lords of Scotland throughout his life and successfully survived their persecution. His clan lands were the hills and glens around Loch Katrine and Loch Lomond and his grave

– which is the subject of a poem by William Wordsworth – is
in Balquhidder.

As well as being active in the complicated politics of his
day and taking part in the intrigues and plots of the nation's
rulers, Rob Roy had responsibility for ordinary people – those
who made up his clan. Although not a chieftain himself he
was related to the head of the MacGregors by birth, and in
effect led the clan for much of his life. Clan Gregor had clashed
with the great lords of Scotland long before Rob Roy's birth.
Their lands lay between the estates of magnates whose sole
plan was to increase them at the cost of their neighbours,
and on the edge of the Highlands themselves. The Mac-
Gregors were therefore in the front line of the cultural and
political changes taking place in the Highlands, at risk from
landowners who wanted their territory; politicians who saw
the Highland people as a threat to the established monarchy
and Protestant religion; and the new middle classes – the
growing breed of bankers, traders and speculators who were
increasingly aware of the huge profits to be made from land
at home and abroad.[3]

To survive this turmoil, Rob Roy played off the forces
threatening him and his clan against each other. On at least
one occasion he was accused of changing sides to save his
own skin, but it has also been argued that his main motive
was to protect the traditional Highland way of life, which was
often considered barbarous and primitive by outside observ-
ers.[4] We can perhaps best understand this legendary version
of the man by comparing him to other tribal leaders who attempted to protect their people from overwhelming social
change, and did so with some success during their life-times.
The great warrior-politicians of the Native American tribes
– Sitting Bull, Crazy Horse and Big Foot – are similar figures, chiefs who also attempted to protect their indigenous
communities against threats to their culture. Like them,
the Rob Roy of this story fought to protect his way of life
with a mixture of war, negotiation and guile; and like them –
although he had some success while he was alive – he ultimately failed, with the language and customs of the Highlands
mostly swept away in the centuries after his death. This

picture of a romantic hero fighting overwhelming odds to preserve something valuable against the forces of greed and exploitation is a very powerful and persuasive one. The parallel to the Native North American chiefs helps place Rob Roy in his historical context, but also, and very importantly for the purposes of studying the 1995 film, it helps explain some of the factors that influenced the way that production was made.

In fact, recent research has revealed a very different picture. The real Rob Roy probably did swindle his creditors and at different points in the Highland uprisings acted as a double agent, both Jacobite rebel and Hanoverian spy. The change from historical fact to the myth we know today has also been traced through the novels, poems, popular ballads and films based on Rob Roy.[5] Some scholars see this as a lack of historical integrity in these stories, including the 1995 film.[6] But an equally valid way to consider it is to see it as proof of the integrity of myth as opposed to historical fact, and of the power of stories to create legends that are politically and culturally meaningful, and so preserve vital messages. The real point of the Rob Roy tale is not about the politics of the era but about the need for human courage in the face of change, and in its portrayal of this belief – essentially a Romantic one – the film remains true to its message.

2. THE SOURCES FOR THE FILM

Texts Based on Rob Roy's Life

Rob Roy was famous in his own lifetime because of the publication of *Rob Roy: Highland Rogue* in 1723, once attributed to Daniel Defoe but now thought to be by the minor writer Elias Brockett.[7] Rob Roy's fame increased after his death with Walter Scott's novel *Rob Roy* (1817), one of the greatest bestsellers of its day. Scott's version made internationally famous the picture of a fearless man doomed to see the end of his own culture, a story which has stayed with us until today. Scott's story went on to be adapted several times for films in the early days of cinema, with feature films made of it in 1911, 1913 and 1922. In 1954 Walt Disney produced another version: *Rob Roy – The Highland Rogue*. The film considered in this study is the most recent fictional version of the tale.

Why has the legend of Rob Roy continued to prove fascinating for so many generations? One reason is probably its sense of adventure, with a bold and resourceful man outwitting powerful enemies despite many dangers and threats. Another is the way the hero tries to preserve honour and integrity in the face of unscrupulous and grasping enemies. A third is that he represents the figure of the admirable outlaw who defends oppressed people against tyrants. Indeed, another key to understanding the Rob Roy myth, as well as comparing him to the Native American leaders, is to see him as a Scottish Robin Hood, protecting the poor and stealing from the rich, and he was certainly compared to that figure both by his contemporaries and by Sir Walter Scott.[8]

As with the legend of Robin Hood, each author or screenwriter who has taken up the story has felt free to change the details to suit his purposes. Despite this, the appeal of each new version remains essentially the same: a heroic, dispossessed man fighting stronger enemies to preserve and protect the things that really matter to him, and to all of us.

The Influences on the 1995 Film

When a screenplay is written, one of the first tasks faced by its creator is to research his story, which of course includes reading or watching all the texts that have been written or produced about the subject before. In the case of *Rob Roy*, when the film's producer, Peter Broughan, and its screenwriter, Alan Sharp, started to develop the idea into a script, it is interesting to consider which earlier stories they used to base their new version on – and which they did not.

There is little sign of Walter Scott's book in the screenplay. Although Scott was one of the most celebrated novelists of the nineteenth century, his popularity declined in the twentieth and fewer adaptations of his books were made. Only one incident in the film – where Rob Roy escapes capture by swimming down a stream – does resemble an event in Scott's book. Another comment by Scott in his 1829 edition of the book, where he compares the Scottish Highlanders to American Red Indians, might also have influenced Sharp.[9] There are few signs of the other films in the 1995 version, and none of the story originally ascribed to Defoe. Other than faint echoes of Scott, Sharp's screenplay owes little to these earlier texts.

A much more direct influence comes from non-fiction. W.H. Murray's *Rob Roy: His Life and Times*, published in 1982, gives an insightful if partisan portrayal of Highland life in Rob Roy's time. Unlike Scott, who was concerned to show how Highland society differed from Lowland Scottish and English culture but also how they might one day work together, Murray champions Highland culture as a separate, unique and proud one, fairer and more democratic than its counterparts in other parts of Britain, but under threat from them. Many of the incidents Murray describes in his book take place in the film. In particular, Murray mentions a fop, Henry Cunninghame, who astonishingly bested the real Rob Roy in a swordfight.[10] It is a passing incident in Murray's book, but a major part of the film. Sharp has clearly picked it up and developed it within his screenplay for his own purposes. *Rob Roy: His Life and Times* has certainly been an important source in shaping the movie.

But beyond this influence, Sharp has told his own version. Like all writers who have dealt with Rob Roy's story he has brought his own vision to it, changing details, characters and facts to suit his message.

Fictionalised versions of real events and people often have little relation to the truth they are based on. Films especially have scant regard for this sort of authenticity, a fact which shows most dramatically in historical movies. *Braveheart*, directed by and starring Mel Gibson and also released in 1995, shows little concern for historical accuracy. But unusually for a screenwriter, Sharp does attempt to portray society, politics and people as they were. He has caught the conflicts and issues of the era, or a version of them. He may have simplified some elements, changed some characters to archetypes and made others (especially Henry Cunninghame, who becomes 'Archibald Cunningham' in the film) much more important than they really were, but his script is an outstanding example of successfully fictionalised history, making the viewer feel that he or she is watching events and adventures that really did happen, as well as being exciting and thoroughly entertaining.

3. WHO MADE *ROB ROY*?

The People Involved in Making a Movie

When we analyse a film, we need to know a good deal about its background and context. This is because the film industry is so large and complex, and also because a film is collaborative, unlike a novel which is usually considered the work of one person.

A screenplay is often regarded as only a blueprint or outline for a film which other people use to guide themselves towards the finished production,and which can be changed along the way.[11] It is sometimes referred to as a 'technical document' to emphasise its practicality and to place it in a relatively low position of importance in the making of the film. The producer, director, lead actors, cinematographers and editors can make more significant creative contributions than the screenwriter. However, some screenwriters are valued more than others and can be given great credibility for their craft and skill, and this is true of *Rob Roy*.

Screenwriter: Alan Sharp

Alan Sharp was born in 1934 in Alyth near Dundee. He was illegitimate and was adopted by a Greenock shipyard worker and his wife when just a few weeks old. He left school at 14 and worked in the shipyards. After working at various jobs, including a brief stint as a detective's assistant and his national service overseas, he returned to Greenock. He got a grant to go to college to become a teacher but gave his wife the money and left to travel instead.

In London, he decided to become a writer. His first book, *A Green Tree in Gedde*, appeared in 1965 to great critical acclaim. It follows the fortunes of four young people, including an incestuous brother and sister, and was banned from Edinburgh public libraries. It was supposed to be part of a trilogy, but after a second book, *The Wind Shifts*, Sharp left the UK for Hollywood.[12]

In the 1970s he wrote the screenplays for five films that are now recognised as among the best of the New American Cinema genre, working with some of Hollywood's greatest directors and actors, including Burt Lancaster, Gregory Peck, George C. Scott, Gene Hackman, Arthur Penn, Robert Aldritch and Sam Peckinpah. New American Cinema, also known as 'The Hollywood Renaissance', was a type of film that emerged in the 1960s in which key American beliefs, such as the 'American Dream' of personal freedom and economic and social optimism, were questioned.[13] Sharp's films – *The Hired Hand, Ulzana's Raid, Night Moves, Billy Two Hats,* and *The First Run* – are gritty in tone and frank and often violent in their subject matter. They overturn or question the audience's assumptions or expectations rather than confirm them, unsettling the conventions of their genres and deliberately avoiding easy entertainment. *Night Moves,* for example, starring Gene Hackman, is an 'anti-detective' thriller where the hero, Moseby (the same name Sharp gave one of his characters in *A Green Tree in Gedde*), finds his skills useless and his life increasingly confused as he is drawn into crime by forces beyond his control. *Ulzana's Raid* with Burt Lancaster portrays the so-called 'Indian Wars' as a savage conflict of attrition rather than the triumph of civilisation over barbarism depicted by the traditional Western.

In part, the nature of Sharp's early screen work is due to the time when these films were made. In the late sixties and early seventies America was struggling with its foreign and home policies. Race riots, the Watergate scandal – which led to the resignation of Richard Nixon as President – political assassinations and the Vietnam War were deeply divisive issues that struck at the roots of American values. People began to question the United States' role abroad and the myths of their own history. *Ulzana's Raid* in particular has been read as a comment on the USA's role in Vietnam (see Section 8).

But in part, too, the scathing tone, the restless action and the mockery of conventional expectations were Sharp's own, and can be seen in his novels. The deliberate disturbance of the conventions of a genre, while also working within them, shown in these earlier films should be borne in mind when analysing *Rob Roy*, where Sharp again pushes at the boundaries of his framing genre, in this case the historical – or 'heritage' – picture, and mingles it with another, the Western. The fact that three of Sharp's best-known films are from the latter genre should also be remembered, as we shall see when we examine the film's representations (see Section 5).

From the late seventies Sharp's career was in US television where he wrote many successful dramas and miniseries, although he did write one more feature, *The Osterman Weekend* (1983), and worked on *The Year of Living Dangerously* with Mel Gibson. But *Rob Roy*'s producer, Peter Broughan, looking for the right writer for his project, chose Sharp because of his track record with Westerns and also because of his standing in Scottish literature.[14] Sharp was commissioned to write the script because Broughan believed that he could provide specific skills and a particular approach. So, whereas in most cases the writer has no power over his screenplay after it has been bought, in this case Sharp's track record, his themes in print and film, and his original nationality were significant factors within the work and made a contribution to the film.

Sharp's books and films have been criticised for their violence and their portrayal of women. Certainly his work is graphic in places and *Rob Roy* is no different in this respect. But in the portrait of gender roles in *Rob Roy* (see Section 6), and especially in Rob's character arc, from proud at the beginning of the film to more humble by its end, the film does differ from the rest of Sharp's material, and so can be seen as a development from his earlier texts.

Since *Rob Roy*, Sharp has written the screenplay for a film which has not yet been produced – *Clarinda* – based on the life of Robert Burns. He also embarked on a thriller based on the death of Christopher Marlowe for Peter Broughan, but withdrew from the project. Most recently, he penned the screenplay for the movie *My Talks with Dean Spanley*, adapted from a novel by Lord Dunsany.

Sharp may have left Greenock long ago (he is reputed to have homes in Los Angeles and elsewhere in Scotland as well as New Zealand), but the town has continued to haunt him. References to it can be found in all his books and films and it has become his signature. In *Rob Roy* it comes when MacDonald is making his way back to Rob's lands with the money borrowed from Killearn, and sees a sign for Greenock by the roadside – that being the port Scots sailed from for America.

Vital as Sharp's screenplay was to the film, however, we need also to consider other people who made the film, especially the producer and the director, who were Scots too, and some of the stars.

Producer: Peter Broughan

Peter Broughan had previously worked with the Scottish Film Council and Granada Television; on *The Draughtsman's Contract* (1982), directed by Peter Greenaway, as a production officer; on *Tutti Frutti* (1987) by John Byrne, as a script editor; and as the producer of Byrne's follow-up series *Your Cheating Heart* (1995). He rose through television production and assistant production roles in film until he was ready to become an independent producer of his own projects. By the early nineties, he was keen to attempt what had never been achieved in Scotland before: the making of a big-budget film planned, produced, set and located in Scotland (see Section 5).

The producer's job is to start, develop, oversee and complete the film, working from the beginnings of an idea through to the distribution of the finished product. He also assembles the money and recruits the people who will be involved. In the case of *Rob Roy*, Broughan was intimately involved with the creation of the story. Inspired by a view of the mountains around Loch Lomond as he was driving home from Glasgow while pondering his next story, Broughan wrote the initial treatment and then set out to employ Alan Sharp as his screenwriter.[15] He visited Sharp at his home in New Zealand and, having persuaded him to accept the job, worked closely with him through the early drafts of the screenplay. He also secured a budget of $30 million from American sources, thus ensuring the film would be one of the major releases of the year. He then set out to find a leading director and a stellar cast.

The track records of people who work in the film business, from actors to directors to technical personnel, are crucial. A film's likelihood of raising sufficient money often depends on who has agreed to lend their name to the project. Importantly from the point of raising funds, Broughan was able to persuade a leading (and Scottish) director, Michael Caton-Jones, to take part. Caton-Jones's presence would certainly have had something to do with stars such as Neeson, Lange and Hurt signing up, as would the quality of the script and the roles on offer. Caton-Jones's reputation was also significant in bringing the project to the attention of United Artists.[16] The fact that this calibre of film industry people wished to support the production guaranteed that it would be a major cinema release, and is a tribute to Broughan's producing skills.

After *Rob Roy*, Broughan continued to produce successful films in Scotland, including *The Flying Scotsman* (2006) starring Johnny Lee Miller and Laura Fraser. He is currently involved with developing another great Scottish story – James Hogg's *The Private Memoirs and Confessions of a Justified Sinner* – for the big screen.

Director: Michael Caton-Jones

Michael Caton-Jones is a leading director of British and American films. Starting with the TV drama *Brond* (1987) adapted from the book of the same name by Frederic Lindsay, he went on to direct the Channel 4 funded film *Scandal* (1989), and then the Hollywood war movie *Memphis Belle* (1990). After *Rob Roy*, he continued to direct films such as *The Jackal* (1997) and *Basic Instinct 2* (2006).

The director's role is to manage the making of the film – to oversee and control all aspects of what the audience sees on the screen, from design to cinematography to working with the actors to editing. He or she has complete power over the film during this stage and must bring it in on time and on budget (extra time on a film set inevitably means spending more money). Directors often leave their own personal stamp on a film and can develop a style that is recognisable to the audience.[17] As the *auteur* or 'author' of the film they can be perceived as at least as important as the stars, and certainly more so than the screenwriter. Alfred Hitchcock and Sam Peckinpah are examples of directors who created their own distinct styles, to the extent that films like *Psycho* or *The*

Wild Bunch are seen as their work rather than the achieve-
ment of any actor or writer.

A director has to have many skills, not the least of which is
the management of people. The size of a feature film should
be considered in order to understand how pressured this
aspect of the job is. A film shot on location must transport a
huge amount of people and equipment to another environment, often a difficult one. It must insure, feed, accommo-
date, dress and supervise the people and protect and use the
equipment. A big budget film can employ as many people as
live in a small town. Extras may be employed by the hundred
or even thousand. Stars must be treated carefully, with due
allowance made for foibles of temperament or personality.
Visas must be provided, contracts negotiated, salaries (in
some cases enormous ones) paid. The difficulties presented
by just one location shoot are often huge. The planning and
preparation of all this, its management and the completion of
the whole process in the editing-room is the responsibility
of the director.

The overall quality of the film, or its *production values*, is
also the director's responsibility, with the actors, cameramen,
set designers, lighting and sound crew, costume designers
and make-up people all depending on his vision. Working
with the actors, the director has the right to change the
script or have parts of it rewritten. Stars are powerful, and
can cause a production to be delayed or even halted if they
are unhappy. As in any other working environment, power
struggles, jealousies, personal problems and politics can become more important than they should be – and it is the
director who has to sort out these difficulties and make sure
the job gets done.

For details of the contributions of the actors, see under each
character in Section 10.

4. THE LANGUAGE OF FILM IN *ROB ROY*

Mise en Scene: Sound, Vision and Editing

Mise en scene is a term used in visual texts which means 'everything in the scene'. It means all the parts of a film which make up its design – the costume, lighting, set design, location, and so on – but it can also mean the visual style of a movie and even its emotional tone.[18] Here it is used with the larger meaning. In order to examine this concept we must look at how technology contributes to making of a movie. This use of equipment – the way sound, visuals and editing are used to create the *mise en scene* – is called the *language* of film.

Sound

Sound is one of the most important parts of a film and is usually underestimated. People tend to remember striking camera shots or quick bursts of images, but the way sound is used to create an effect is equally important, and often more subtle. It can suggest atmosphere, delineate character, build tension, heighten climaxes, and rouse the audience's emotions: shock, scare, excite or quieten them.

We can consider film sound in two ways: **diegetic** and **non-diegetic**. (The word *diegesis* means telling a story through a device such as a narrator, as opposed to *mimesis*, which means enacting or showing it through action, characters, events and dialogue.[19]) Diegetic music helps tell the story by occurring within the narrative of the film. It comes from a source seen in the film such as a radio, a record player, a musical instrument, a juke-box or an orchestra in a concert hall. The characters of the film can hear it. Non-diegetic music is not part of the narrative, not attributable to a source in the film, and is unheard by the characters. Both diegetic and non-diegetic sound can be used throughout a film in many different ways

In *Rob Roy*, the band who play at the ceilidh (who are Capercaillie, a real band) provide an example of diegetic sound. The band members are people within the film whom the other characters see and hear. The young woman who sings the haunting Gaelic song 'Ailein Duinn, Ò Hì, Shiùblainn Leat' (played by Karen Matheson, Capercaillie's lead singer) is also a real character within the film and so her song is diegetic.

An example of non-diegetic sound is the movie's opening shot, where we see the Highlanders appear against a backdrop of beautiful scenery and hear music with a striking resemblance to the Native American rhythms. Stirring non-diegetic music is also heard at the start of the scene where Cunningham duels with Guthrie. Romantic non-diegetic music plays when Rob returns to Mary after killing Tam Sibbald and washes in the loch (recalling the legend of the selkie, a mythical beast in Scottish folklore that is half-man, half-seal and is often associated with sensuality – ironically echoed by Cunningham's arrival at the same place later, when he too comes from the water). Non-diegetic music is used throughout the film to suggest colour, atmosphere and emotion – to play the audience's emotions just as you would play an instrument.

The music in *Rob Roy*, which was created by leading film composer Carter Burwell, uses a range of styles. Big, sweeping melodies reminiscent of classical American films tell us that this is a large and in some ways quite traditional movie. These passages are romantic, historical and have a consciously 'Hollywood' air. The Scottish element emerges with the use of bagpipes and Highland lilts in the soundtrack similar to those used in classic films set in Scotland, such as *Brigadoon*. This is updated in other parts of the film, such as the moment when the diegetic Scottish or Celtic folk music of Capercaillie is used, which makes that part of the soundtrack more authentic and contemporary. Mixed in with this is a much more unusual type of music for the subject: Native American elements, which seem more suitable for a Western. The analogy is clear: the Highlanders are being compared to the Native North Americans and their histories of persecution and resistance are being deliberately paralleled.

Another type of sound is sound effects ('SFX'). These are added after the real sound of the film has been recorded, usually to heighten dramatic moments. The roar Rob gives as he hacks Cunningham in two and the slithering sound of steel

at the moments swords are drawn have been added during the editing process to emphasise moments of tension or
release. Much of their effect comes from the fact that the
audience is unaware these sounds are being used to manipulate their reactions.

Silence is not usually considered a sound element, but it is
very important – especially at moments of extreme tension
or in the middle of a scene where the atmosphere suddenly
changes. In the crowded tavern, as Guthrie tries to persuade
Killearn to hire him to track down Rob, the hubbub suddenly
dies away. The crowd parts in silence to show Rob. Non-
diegetic music starts up, pipes over an echoing drum, creating
apprehension. We know that violence is close. The drumbeat
continues as Rob confronts Killearn and Guthrie intervenes,
swelling to a bass note (implying darkness and death) and
joining with the pipes and drum until it becomes one long
drawn-out note on strings, the classic noise of tension, as Rob
and Guthrie face each other. Sound effects of ringing steel
emphasise the violence as Guthrie attacks only to be swiftly
despatched by Rob. So in this short sequence, both diegetic
and non-diegetic sound – silence, music and sound effects –
have created a tapestry behind the action that enlarges and
enhances the drama. Sound can be used throughout a movie
in ways like these to create deep emotional resonance.

Dialogue is an extremely important part of any movie.
A screenwriter has far fewer tools at his disposal to help
him tell his story than a novelist. Only the visuals and the
dialogue are available, and other people control the visuals.
Dialogue in screenplays therefore has to work much harder
than in other media. It must suggest character, seem authentic, be unique, and tell the audience as much as necessary
about the plot, setting and period. Often in films it is spare,
pared back to the bone, but writers will also seek to leave
their own individual stamp on their screenplays, and so may
develop a certain style in their characters' speech.

The dialogue in *Rob Roy* is a triumph. Sharp's style, a mix
of powerful concrete images and everyday speech, can be dis-
cerned in the film's dialogue in exactly the same way as in
his earlier works, such as *A Green Tree in Gedde* – indeed, he

occasionally uses the same lines.[20] He suggests the Highlanders' distinct culture through their speech, often having them use animal imagery to show their closeness to the natural world, in contrast to the Lowlanders' mode of talking, which is much more matter-of-fact and mostly concerned with the mundane facts of money and worth. More than this, he has created dialogue that seems realistic for the period and understandable to a modern audience. It is an approximation of eighteenth century speech that seems authentic and allows the actors wonderfully evocative lines, an intelligent and original use of dialogue that is rare in contemporary films.

Examples:
   '... and there he was hung on the end of my dirk like meat.' (Rob Roy on killing Tam Sibbald)

   'He ravished her?'
   'I would put it no higher than surprised.' (Cunningham talking to Betty about his mother)

   'You think me such a puppet that I would put my head in a noose fashioned from my own dishonour?' (Mary to Killearn)

   'There is something here that I do not see. Killearn and you have some hand in matters that is hid from sight. This tells me that you are in cash. Yet I know you are without means.'
   'Gaming, your Lordship. The cards favoured.' (Montrose and Cunningham.)

   All aspects of the film's sound, including the dialogue, therefore contribute to the film's distinct emotional tone, its *mise en scene.*

Camera: Distance, Angle, Movement
In films, the camera is the most vital part of the director's equipment. Film camerawork differs from television camerawork in being larger, more sweeping, more consciously artis-

tic and much more expensive. While television tends to focus on character, film visuals are richer and more complex. They also have the greatest impact on the audience. With sound, the camera is the main way of telling the story in a film, much more so than the script. Screenwriters therefore learn to let the visuals tell the story by avoiding unnecessary explanation and using only minimal dialogue.

Michael Caton-Jones uses the camera in *Rob Roy* to do all these things. The beautiful scenery is shown in all its grandeur and colour and the battle-scenes and the swordfight are fast-paced and exciting. Like all directors, he uses the camera in particular ways to achieve the effects he wants. Some of these uses and effects follow:

Camera angle: the angle of the camera is one way of creating an emotional impact on the viewer. High-angle, when the shot is taken of a character from above, can make that person look vulnerable or threatened. Low-angle, when a character is seen from below, makes the person seem large, threatening and dominant. A professional director knows how to use these camera shots to produce this and many other effects.

Camera shot: camera shot means the distance between the subject and the camera. It can vary from a Long Shot that shows a huge amount of landscape (commonly called an Establishing Shot, used at the start of a film to establish the world in which the film is set), to an Extreme Close-Up, where we see only a detail of a character's face such as the eyes.

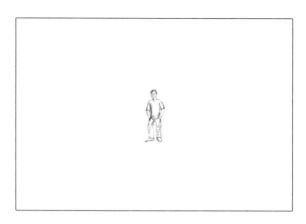

Extreme Long Shot (ELS): The camera is placed at a great distance from the character(s), showing them in their setting. Often used to show the landscape, *mise en scene* or 'world' at the opening of a film, and often called an Establishing Shot because it places the characters in the most significant location in the story.

Long Shot (LS): Shows a character's whole figure but in more detail than the Extreme Long Shot. Used to portray a character in his/her place or in relation to a symbolic landmark. A Long Shot often introduces a character in a film for the first time. It can also act as an Establishing Shot.

Medium Long Shot (MLS): Shows a character's whole figure but less of its *mise en scene*. More detail of a character is seen here than the ELS or LS but it can still include some smaller parts of the setting.

Medium Shot (MS): Shows the human figure roughly from the knees to just above the head. Gives still more detail of a character than the Long Shot and can retains some small parts of his/her *mise en scene*.

Medium Close Up (MCU): Shows the figure from mid-chest to the top of the head. Gives much more detail of a character. The frame of this shot can include two people talking and is often used to show a pair of characters in conversation (dualogue).

Close Up (CU): Shows the figure's head and shoulders. This shot is used to show a character's emotions or reactions at strong moments of drama.

Extreme Close Up (ECU): Shows extreme detail, for example the full human face or an even smaller area such as the eyes. This shot is used to show intensely dramatic moments, and emotions such as terror.

Camera movement: as well as angle and shot, the director can move a camera while it is shooting to create an effect. Methods of moving cameras include helicopters, cranes and tracks. The Steadicam is a camera that can be strapped to a cameraman's body and move as he walks without jolting. Hand-held cameras that take wobbly, jerky shots are used to create an impression of informality or to make the action seem more real.

Editing

When all the film footage has been shot, the process of editing begins, and it is at this stage that the director really makes his story. Using digital technology, the shots can be placed in any order, cut, enlarged or changed, sounds added, music introduced, and the pace of each part of the film adjusted to suit the action. An action sequence will tend to be fast, a romantic scene will usually be slow. The editor controls the speed at which events unfold, and so influences the audience's reaction.

A Sequence from Rob Roy

Let's look in some detail at how Michael Caton-Jones, the film's director, influenced the audience's reaction, using the camera, the sound and the editing, in a short sequence from *Rob Roy*.

1. **Shot**: Long
   Sound: Rob Roy's gasps, clash of steel
   Editing: 2–3 second shot to show the pace of the battle: bursts of energy punctuated by pauses as Rob tries to recover his strength

2. **Shot**: Medium
   Sound: Diegetic: Rob Roy's exhausted gasps, Cunningham's steadily pacing footsteps
   Editing: Shot lasts 3–4 seconds to emphasise the slow, deliberate way Cunningham is stalking Rob and draining his strength

3. Shot: Medium
   Sound: Diegetic: Rob's gasps, Cunningham's footsteps
   Editing: as with Shot 2
   Camera Movement: Camera pans down to show Rob's exhausted stance and Cunningham's more graceful movements

4. Shot: Medium
   Sound: Diegetic: Rob's gasps
   Editing: Shot lasts 1 second to show Rob's expression as he stares at his adversary and licks his lips in fear

5. Shot: Medium
   Sound: Diegetic: Rob's gasps, Cunningham's footsteps
   Editing: Shot lasts 1 second as Cunningham stares at
   Rob as a hunter studies his prey

6. Shot: Long
   Sound: Diegetic: Rob's gasps etc.
   Editing: 1 second to re-establish place and the positioning
   of the characters in relation to each other
   Camera Angle: Low, emphasising the arched roof of the
   duelling room and the way it now seems like a trap
   Composition: balanced: group of characters on the right
   are balanced by windows and lights on the left: roof-arches
   define the room's shape: Rob and Cunningham at the
   centre

7. Shot: Medium Close Up
Sound: Rob's gasps
Editing: Shot lasts 1 second to emphasise Rob's increasing despair and exhaustion

8. Shot: Medium Close Up
Sound: Rob's gasps
Editing: Shot lasts 1 second to emphasise Cunningham's increasing confidence

9. Shot: Medium
Sound: Diegetic: Rob's gasps
Editing: 0.25 second shot to show Argyll's anxious reaction to the way the duel is developing

10. Shot: Medium Close Up
Sound: Diegetic: Rob's gasps
Editing: 0.5 second shot to show Rob's increasingly distressed state

11. **Shot**: Long
   Sound: Diegetic: Rob's gasps, sword tip being dragged over the stone floor (SFX)
   Editing: Shot lasts 1–2 seconds to re-establish setting and to emphasise Rob's exhausted movements

12. **Shot**: Medium Close Up
   Sound: Diegetic: Rob's gasps, sword tip being dragged over the stone floor (SFX)
   Editing: Shot lasts 3–4 seconds to show Rob's staggering movements and exhausted expression

13. Shot: Medium Close Up
   Sound: Diegetic: silence
   Editing: Shot lasts 1 second to display Cunningham's increasing self-assurance as Rob grows weaker

14. Shot: Medium Close Up
   Sound: Diegetic: Rob's gasps
   Editing: Shot lasts 1 second to show Rob's despair as he gets ready for one final attack

15. Shot: Medium
Sound: Diegetic: Rob's roar as he attacks
Editing: Shot lasts for 0.5 seconds to show the speed of the attack

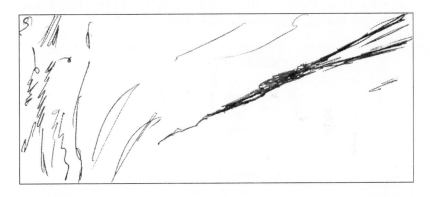

16. Shot: Close Up
Sound: Diagetic: tearing sound of flesh and cloth
Editing: shot lasts 0.05 seconds to show the speed of the action as Cunningham inflicts the wound on Rob

17. Shot: Medium Long
    Sound: Diagetic: Rob's groan as he is wounded, noise of swords clashing, Rob's being dropped (SFX)
    Editing: shot lasts 0.5 seconds to show the effect of the wound on Rob, i.e. the way he drops his sword and falls to his knees, apparently defeated

18. Shot: Close Up
    Sound: Diegetic: Rob's gasps as he lies on hands and knees, wounded
    Editing: shot lasts 0.5 second to show the gloating pleasure Cunningham takes in Rob's defeat

19. Shot: Medium Close Up
   Sound: Diegetic: Rob's gasps, Cunningham's footsteps
   Editing: shot lasts 0.5 seconds to show Rob's pain and
   helplessness

20. Shot: Medium Close Up
   Sound: Diegetic: sounds of Rob in pain
   Editing: Shot lasts 0.5 seconds as Montrose glances at
   Argyll in triumph

21. **Shot**: Long
    Sound: Diegetic: Rob's groans of pain, Cunningham's footsteps
    Editing: Shot lasts 2–3 seconds to show Rob slumped on the ground and Cunningham moving in for the kill

22. **Shot**: Medium Close Up
    Sound: Diegetic: Rob gasps as the blade touches his throat; Non-Diegetic: an unexpectedly ominous note of music sounds
    Editing: Shot lasts 2 seconds to show Rob at his most vulnerable as Cunningham uses his sword to lift his victim's head

23. Shot: Medium
   Sound: Diegetic: Rob gasps as his head is forced up; Non-Diegetic: the ominous note rises and swells
   Editing: Shot lasts 4 seconds to show that the moment of greatest drama has come; Rob seems completely at Cunningham's mercy as the latter stares down at his victim
   Camera Angle: Low angle emphasises Cunningham's dominance over Rob

24. Shot: Medium
   Sound: Diegetic: Rob's gasps; Non-Diegetic: the music rises further
   Editing: Shot lasts 2 seconds to show Rob's helplessness and to establish the position of the dukes and their servants in the background in relation to the duellists
   Camera Angle: Level with Rob, showing his apparent submission to Cunningham

Rob Roy is made up of sequences like these, all of which, stitched together into a complete story, make up its *mise en scene*.

5. *ROB ROY* AS A REPRESENTATION OF SCOTLAND

Is *Rob Roy* a 'Scottish' film?

Is *Rob Roy* really a Scottish film, and does it matter? To consider this aspect of the production we need to consider a few facts about Scotland and about films in general.

Scotland does not have a strong tradition in the cinema. Many films have been set in it, but films made by Scottish people about their own lives or history were few and far between until the 1970s, when some enterprising young producers and directors took matters into their own hands.[21] Some of the productions they made, such as *Gregory's Girl* and *Local Hero* by Bill Forsyth, were successful and inspired others to make films, and many talented Scottish people have worked and still work in the film industry. But without an indigenous cinema industry at home all Scottish actors, directors and producers have inevitably had to go abroad to work. There have been exceptions to this, but the huge majority of Scots who have achieved great success in films (and in almost all other media) have achieved it outside Scotland.

Scottish cinema is not alone in this respect. One of the struggles faced by Scottish people in any of the arts is that of making a distinct tradition, and so a thriving culture. Scotland's historical position, as a nation within an Empire that has nevertheless preserved a considerable proportion of its identity, means that at different times in its history and in different ways it has both won and lost from its situation. In the early and mid twentieth century its arts such as theatre, literature, painting and film often struggled to make much impact, even in Scotland. With increasing confidence and a growing feeling of national identity in the later twentieth century, some of these arts, especially literature, enjoyed a great upsurge of popularity, with some Scottish authors becoming well known at home and overseas.

Film is different from other arts because of the amount of money involved. It is a high-risk business, where producers have to raise large amounts of cash from investors, persuading them to risk it on what no one can really guarantee –

public taste. It is not surprising that it is a conservative industry where what has proved popular is usually preferred to something more risky or unusual. It is therefore difficult to bring about any change in the industry or to make a new kind of film. So although successful films in and about Scotland were made from the late 1970s onwards, including some very famous and successful ones, such as *My Childhood* (1977), *Braveheart* (1995) and *Trainspotting* (1996), they tended to be individual events rather than what might be called an industry.

But what makes a film 'Scottish' in the first place? Is it the use of a Scottish star, or the fact that the production is made in Scotland, or that it has a Scottish setting? Is there a particular style of Scottish filmmaking, and do distinct Scottish themes emerge? There are many debates and different points of view. In *Rob Roy*'s case, the stars were Irish, American and English. The money to make it was raised in America. It was filmed on location in Scotland (in contrast to *Braveheart*, which for tax reasons was filmed in Ireland). So how Scottish is it?

This is a complex area of debate, but we can consider two traditions in Scottish film to see what makes *Rob Roy* special. On the one hand, there is the sort of major blockbuster Hollywood production that visits Scotland to make a film or set it here, spinning a fantasy to create an entertaining spectacle and using a huge budget. The stars, producer, director and budget will come from Hollywood. *Braveheart* and *Brigadoon* are examples of this. Scotland will not necessarily be the location (*Brigadoon* was made in a Hollywood studio, its director, having visited Scotland, claiming that he couldn't find anything that looked particularly Scottish there) but it will be the concept. These films will be popular all over the world, including Scotland. On the other hand, there are low-budget films that attempt to show us Scotland as it is, their aim being to shock, disturb or show true social circumstances. *My Childhood* by Bill Douglas is one of these. *My Childhood* shows a grim place, a ruined post-industrial landscape where elderly women and neglected children try to survive in a world that ignores them. It is a masterpiece of poetic filmmaking, a truly groundbreaking film, but made as it was for a tiny amount of money and shown only in arts cinemas, the fact is that the majority of Scottish people will probably never see it, and no investor will put money into such a film again.

What is unique about *Rob Roy* is that it was an attempt by a Scottish producer and director to make a major Hollywood-style epic picture about Scotland and in Scotland, controlling the production from Scotland itself. This is important because it tried to break with the split between the two types of film described above. Instead of trying to invent a style of picture-making that was unique or new to Scotland, it acknowledged that the most popular form of cinema in Scotland is and always has been the Hollywood one – indeed, it used one of Hollywood's greatest genres, the Western, as its model. But it also sought to establish control over the production from Scotland, employing major stars and bringing them to the film rather than importing the project from abroad. It also showed some concern for accuracy, for authenticity, thus echoing Bill Douglas's desire to recreate on film the world he had grown up in.

It is this fact that gives *Rob Roy* much of its unique identity and tone. Its ambition to set a precedent in Scottish film by trying to bring two opposing kinds of film practice together in one work should be remembered when we consider its other unique aspects, such as the way it shows Scotland, the way it depicts gender, and its genre(s) and themes.

Scotland in Film – Representations of Scotland

What are representations and why are they important? A representation is literally what is shown, an image on the screen that depicts what the audience sees.[22] But, of course, the audience sees it the way the filmmaker depicts it, using tricks like lighting, camerawork, makeup and costume. In fictional stories, this is also affected by things like acting, narrative, genre, the expectations of the audience, and so on.

So what we see on a screen is not reality but an artificial version of it, an imitation. This copy, or representation, can be used to manipulate the audience's emotions and make it believe the message the film is delivering. This is why representations in films and on television can be so powerful, and what makes the study of them so important. They express the filmmaker's *ideology*, or the set of values behind the film he or she is making. And to some extent every filmmaker sets out to influence the audience and 'sell' it those central ideals.

Scotland has been depicted in film for as long as movies have been made. It was well known in fictional stories at the start of cinema, used to evoke exoticism to an overseas audience, or nostalgia if they had Scottish connections.[23] Early filmmakers, who looked around for proven stories to make into films so as to minimise the risk, found that Scotland provided them with a distinct, ready-made and highly visual world.[24]

But the traditional representations of Scotland used by these pioneers of cinema (castles, kilts, sporrans, whisky and strange accents) were far from the truth, and this was of concern to critics who felt that they were stereotypes. These images owed much to the Romantic portrayal of Scotland which had been made famous by Walter Scott, and was criticised by people who felt that it was a distorted view.[25] A film like *Brigadoon*, for example, which showed a place of magical mountains and glens where happy Highlanders danced and sang, could be accused of ignoring the real social conditions of the Highlands. This Romantic portrait of Scotland seemed to many just as misleading and repressive as the Kailyard, or cabbage-patch, tradition – that being the mid to late nineteenth century period of Scottish literature that was seen as its lowest point, a mixture of sentimentality and nostalgia that patronised both its characters and its readers.

But the argument about how to show Scotland in films has changed in the last twenty years or so. There has been some reconsideration of the Kailyard period and much more interest and research in Scottish history generally. Instead of condemning the tartan image of Scotland wholesale as an unacceptable stereotype, writers, critics and historians now tend to agree on a much wider and more tolerant view of Scottish history. The Scotland of the past is now seen as a complex, multi-cultural and multi-layered society, with Walter Scott's Romanticism and Highland culture's role within it placed more in their context.

Rob Roy attempts to show the popular view and one of the legendary figures of Scottish culture in a way that is historically realistic (or as near to it as possible), but also entertaining and in the Hollywood tradition. Like the earlier representations of Scotland, and like *Braveheart*, castles, kilts, swords and mountains are present in abundance. But like other films that concern themselves with realism, there is no attempt at sweetness. Genuine social conflicts of the period – the sternness of the Calvinists (mentioned by Coll at the ceilidh), the schism between Highlander and Lowlander, the changes to Highland culture, the growth of commercialism and the power struggle over the succession to the throne – are outlined sharply without affecting the power of the movie.

The originality and realism of this representation of Scotland can be seen most dramatically in the scene entitled 'Atrocity at Inversnaid', where Rob's house is burned and Mary is raped. To the motifs of the traditional and even stereotypical Scottish scene (beautiful scenery, misty air, a simple life lived close to the natural world) it brings graphic violence and brutality. It shows a picture of Scotland which neither denies its Romantic tradition nor its darker history.

6. *ROB ROY* AND GENDER

Another tradition of Hollywood that is questioned in *Rob Roy* is to do with gender. Conventional Scottish culture is highly masculine. Women play secondary roles in the stereotypical Scottish story, where males are tough fighters who value physical prowess, manhood and honour – a tradition that perhaps springs from Scotland's struggle to be recognised as a distinct nation. The masculine is prized above all (an example of this can be seen in the 1990 film *The Big Man*, also starring Liam Neeson).

The same is true of the traditional Western, where male values are tested and portrayed throughout the narrative while female roles are restricted to romance, children and the home. In many Westerns women barely appear. The men may fall in love, raise families and enjoy the comforts of home, but these issues are usually handled in one or two scenes or a few lines of dialogue. Most of the story is spent in harsh, gritty settings where trials like gunfights, pursuits, wars, killings and crime are acted out, and where men prove themselves in terms of their strength, speed and stamina.

At first it seems that *Rob Roy* continues this tradition. Rob is the archetypal masculine hero: strong, hardy, skilful and handsome, a famous tracker and a mighty warrior. He has to endure terrible trials alone, leaving home to fight soldiers and other powerful opponents in the wilderness. Meanwhile Mary looks after his children and home. But in fact, *Rob Roy* breaks with the traditional representation of gender in a significant way, and the move from the masculine to the feminine is one of the main progressions within the film, constituting Rob's 'character arc' – or development – from beginning to end of the movie. Feminists have long argued that there is a parallel in traditional masculine texts between landscape and the female body.[26] Territorial conquest and the taming of 'nature' (e.g. untilled land, wildlife and hostile natives) is inevitably symbolised by the subjugation of the female and the confirmed dominance of the male. *Rob Roy* breaks with this stereotype. As the story unfolds Rob comes to regret the fact that he left Mary to fight alone. He realises he should have valued what he loved more dearly, and not been so proud. His character development is from honourable and isolated to more accepting and caring, from trusted leader to loving husband. The common narrative *trope* – or typical pattern – of civilisation being wrestled from the wilderness by masculine strengths has been changed to civilisation preserved in the natural world by female values.

The women in the film have smaller roles but they play more than supporting parts. They are also strong in different ways. The woman who follows Tam Sibbald's band of broken men is the only one with the courage to try to fight Rob. The idea of female courage continues with Betty. She illustrates the fate of innocent working-class girls caught up in circumstances beyond her control. Met by Killearn leaving Cunningham's room, she is physically and verbally abused by him (he takes liberties with the girls of the household because he knows he has power over them). Betty hopes that Cunningham will honour her, become her husband and give her baby his 'name'; but Cunningham betrays her, Killearn informs on her and she is sacked. Even so, she shows bravery and resourcefulness in facing them both in Montrose's garden at night and demanding that her unborn child be made legitimate.

Illegitimacy is not just the curse of the child but of the mother too. The social stigma, the resulting poverty and fear of the future combine to create too heavy a burden for Betty to bear, and this is what leads to her suicide. But despite her humble beginnings and the abuse of unscrupulous employers, she nevertheless has dared to dream of a better life for herself and her child. Her death is not the act of a coward but a tragedy to be mourned. The implication is that it is a fate that befalls many young women.

Rob Roy shows plainly that women have harder lives than men. 'It's a hard thought, that men make the quarrels but women and weans bear them,' Argyll says to Mary when she comes to ask for his protection. Hard though it may be, he is quite prepared to cast Mary off rather than get involved in a fight with Montrose until he learns that Montrose tried to involve Rob in a plot against him. Cunningham's aristocratic mother conceives a bastard child who will never amount

to anything. Betty loses her job as a maid and kills herself.
These representations of female difficulties and the strength
to endure them are expressed most clearly of all in the character of Mary (see Section 10). Raped, humiliated, her home
destroyed, pregnant and unsure if she can live with the
shame, she survives, although even Rob lets her down when
he departs for the hills.

But it is in the character of Archibald Cunningham that
the myth of the masculine is most questioned. Cunningham's
claim to masculinity itself is called into question from the
moment he appears: 'So Mr Cunningham, what are these
principal sins that so distress your mother? Dice? Drink?
Or are you a buggerer of boys?' Argyll asks him contemptuously. Cunningham is different from the standard ma-
chismo of Highland society, and also from men portrayed in
Westerns and traditional Hollywood movies. His accent is a
parody of the refined; he has a mincing manner of speech.
He is affected and, beside Highlanders like Guthrie, almost
effeminate. His dress and his mannerisms are a parody, deliberately flamboyant and showy. His style of sword fighting
seems like ballet against Guthrie's. And yet the traditional
male qualities of brute strength and physical intimidation
are no match for Cunningham. His almost female qualities
of grace and restrained aggression completely overpower the
Highlanders, who are helpless against them. He proves himself a better soldier, leader and warrior than anyone, even
their greatest leader, Rob Roy. Cunningham's lethal personality springs from the dishonour and isolation he endured
in childhood. (His mother never appears in the movie except
as a miniature portrait worn by her son.) He overturns the
Highlanders' assumptions, and ours, that masculine striving
and an agreed code of behaviour will win the day. Rob, completely outwitted and beaten in every respect, only succeeds
when he cheats and breaks the rules of the duel, shown when
he grabs the tip of the victorious Cunningham's sword, preventing the swordsman from delivering the final blow. Rob
has learned not to live by a masculine code. And this in turn
echoes his growth from the male to the female, away from
the code of honour towards the manner of love.

7. *ROB ROY*: STRUCTURE

The classic Hollywood structure of a feature film is three Acts. Derived from theatre, the mainstream Hollywood story therefore has three recognisable phases. There are many theories about how a story is best told, and not all of them agree, but because so much money is involved in making a movie, rules have sprung up which producers expect scripts to follow and which screenwriters must master. The key aim is to manipulate the audience's emotions. It should be made to laugh, cry, feel love, hate and anger and share the feelings and experiences of the characters.

The first phase, or Act One, is the introduction to the story, setting up the characters and the world they live in. It introduces us to the 'normality' of the characters' existence. It is the second longest Act, and it will end with an action, sometimes called 'The Inciting Incident', which changes everything in this world and creates another, more dangerous place through which the most important characters (or more often, a single character, the protagonist or 'hero') must travel on a quest.[27]

Act Two deals with the challenges, pitfalls, disappointments, downfalls and triumphs experienced by the hero during his journey. He will have to face a foe, the antagonist, who may either be a character or a force, who prevents him from getting what he wants. There will also be many other trials, opponents and conflicts. The more confrontations, oppositions and reversals of fortune there are for the hero, the more gripping the story. The audience should be kept on the edge of its seat by the overwhelming odds, unexpected events, twists and turns of the plot and the amount of pain and difficulty the hero faces. His struggles should rise in importance, danger and tension through a series of crises to a main crisis near the end of the Act.[28] The gravest crisis of all is death, which the hero often faces in some way, or even endures. Act Two is the longest phase of the film.

Act Three is relatively short and must provide a conclusion, and also something unexpected, bringing the audience to a climax which is not necessarily more overwhelming than

in Act Two but which is more important. It should round off
the tale. Sometimes called the Resolution or Restoration, this
phase resolves the drama and restores the world the hero left
at the start, or makes a new one. It is the end of the quest.

The events of the film in the classic structure

The following section sums up the key events in *Rob Roy*
within the classic film structure. For more information about
how to write a script, see the bibliography at the end of this
book.

Act One

Rob Roy and a group of his followers track some cattle-thieves
led by the broken man Tam Sibbald through the glens (NOR-
MALITY). The thieves have taken the cattle from Rob who
looks after them for the Marquis of Montrose, a great land
owner. Rob decides to talk to the thieves rather than attack
them (NORMALITY). Next morning he challenges Tam Sibbald: he can die honourably here or on the scaffold. Sibbald
attacks Rob and is killed. Rob and his followers take the cattle back to return to Montrose (NORMALITY).

The Marquis of Montrose and the Duke of Argyll meet
at the duelling-place. Argyll's champion, Will Guthrie, and
Montrose's new champion, Archibald Cunningham, agree to
do battle while their masters wager on them (NORMALITY).
As the fighting commences the two lords discuss matters at
court, especially the succession and the intrigue surrounding
who will be the next monarch (NORMALITY). Argyll accuses
Montrose of trying to blacken his character at court. Cunningham's effete mannerisms are mocked as he prepares to
fight, but he easily beats Guthrie, outwitting and overpower-
ing him (this sequence parallels the swordfight at the end of
the film), and Argyll loses the bet (NORMALITY).

Rob Roy and his followers drive the stolen cattle back to
Rob Roy's lands. Rob sees that the elderly and young of his
clan are hungry and sick, and decides to feed them with one
of the recovered cattle, blaming its loss on the thieves. He
returns home, washes in the sea, tucks in his children, and
joins Mary in bed (NORMALITY).

At Montrose's castle, the Marquis's factor Killearn wakes up Cunningham after mocking and abusing the maid Betty, who has spent the night in Cunningham's room. Killearn tells Cunningham that Montrose knows of his debts. Back on the MacGregor lands, Rob tells Mary about his plan to borrow money from Montrose so that his clan can prosper. (NORMALITY)

In a private interview, Montrose upbraids Cunningham about his debts. Cunningham is his guest, he points out, not a member of his household. Rob Roy, who has been waiting outside, is next to be seen. Montrose strikes a deal with Rob: he will lend him £1,000 Scots for the purchase of cattle, but Rob's lands will be forfeit if he does not pay it back (NORMALITY). Later at a town tavern Rob Roy signs for the money. He is challenged by Argyll's defeated champion Will Guthrie over the death of Tam Sibbald, but refuses to fight. Back at Montrose's castle Cunningham tells Betty he doesn't know who his father is. He is illegitimate and penniless. Betty tells Cunningham she is pregnant (NORMALITY).

Killearn comes to Cunningham's door and tells him of MacGregor's loan. Stealing it is an easy and safe way for Cunningham and Killearn to make money. Rob Roy announces to his clan that he has taken out a loan which will help them survive, and calls for a ceilidh (NORMALITY). Alan MacDonald, Rob Roy's friend and guest, waits for the money at the tavern, and is paid by Killearn in coin, not with a Note of Credit. MacDonald leaves as the ceilidh begins and is stalked, then chased by Cunningham. He is hunted down like a wild beast in the woods, and the money stolen (INCITING INCIDENT). MacDonald's body is weighted down and sunk in a loch.

Rob knows he is in trouble. His lands are forfeit and he has no other way to pay off the debt. Everyone else believes Mac-Donald has stolen the money, but Rob cannot. He presents himself to Montrose to ask for another loan. Montrose demands that Rob betrays Argyll as payment of his debt. Rob refuses. In rage, Montrose tries to have Rob arrested, but Rob draws his dagger, overpowers Cunningham and flees. He is on the run, a hunted man.

This is the end of the first phase of the drama: the old way of things has changed and the hero has entered a new, more dangerous world.

Act Two

Rob packs up and leaves his house despite Mary's pleas and arguments (CONFRONTATION). He thinks she will be safe and that Montrose's argument is only with him. He takes to the hills leaving his senior clansman Coll in charge. Montrose sends Cunningham and Killearn out with troops to hunt Rob down at any cost. Rob must be returned 'broken, but not dead' (OPPOSITION). Coll warns Alasdair Roy, Rob's young brother, to keep his watch. That night Rob sleeps in the open, Mary at home, and Alasdair by the shore. The young man's lack of discipline lets Montrose's troops through to the loch (REVERSAL). Cunningham attacks Rob's home from the loch, the troops arriving in boats (REVERSAL). They kill the stock and set fire to the cottage (CONFRONTATION). Cunningham violates Mary in front of Killearn (CONFRON-TATION). Alasdair arrives too late to help as the troops leave. Alasdair realises the truth about the violence inflict-ed on Mary. She swears him to silence. Rob must not know about the rape (REVERSAL).

Cunningham reports back to Montrose: Rob Roy is not yet caught but has been given 'such an affront to his High-land honour' that he is sure to come looking for revenge (CONFRONTATION). Montrose quizzes Cunningham and Killearn about MacDonald's disappearance and the theft of the money (REVERSAL). Killearn warns Cunningham that Montrose suspects, but Cunningham knows Montrose has gained Rob Roy's lands for hardly any money. Betty accosts Cunningham in the castle gardens (CONFRONTATION), but he denies any responsibility for her now that she has been dismissed from service. Meanwhile Rob has called the Gregorach – the MacGregors – together for a council of war (OPPOSITION) and argues that the best way forward is not to meet Montrose's aggression head on, but to hit back at his purse. The clansmen are to thieve his cattle and rents (CONFRONTATION).

Rob takes his family to a new home, a remote cottage in a distant glen. He blames himself for not defending Mary (RE-VERSAL) but she says he would be dead if he had stayed. Later, Betty comes to Mary and tells her about the conversation she overheard between Killearn and Cunningham (OP-POSITION). Mary knows the truth now. She tells Rob, who swears vengeance. In the town tavern Killearn is talking with Guthrie. Guthrie wants to work for Montrose and track Rob Roy down (REVERSAL). Rob appears (CONFRONTA-TION), kills Guthrie and kidnaps Killearn (REVERSAL). Rob takes Killearn to his hideout and tells Alasdair to fetch Betty. He means to try Killearn as if he is a prisoner of war (REVERSAL). Alasdair tells Mary to fetch Betty but Betty has hung herself in despair (REVERSAL). Mary and Alasdair join Rob on the island. Mary talks to Killearn alone: Killearn guesses that Mary is pregnant as a result of the rape and tries to blackmail her (CONFRONTATION/OPPOSITION). In fury, Mary stabs Killearn (REVERSAL). Killearn staggers out to the loch and is drowned by Alasdair Roy (OPPOSI-TION). Mary seems almost about to tell Rob of the rape but is prevented by Alasdair coming back and saying Killearn is dead (REVERSAL). Rob knows Montrose's anger will know no bounds (CONFRONTATION). He tells Alasdair to sink Killearn's body in the loch.

Montrose is furious at his loss of earnings, the raids on his territory and rents and the abduction of his factor (RE-VERSAL/CONFRONTATION). He instructs Cunningham to stop these affronts to his good name. Cunningham attacks a Highland township and burns the cottages (OPPOSI-TION). Rob Roy and his followers watch from nearby. Rob decides not to attack but Alasdair shoots at the soldiers, giving away the Highlanders' position (REVERSAL). The soldiers pursue the Highlanders who try to hide in the mist. Alasdair is hit and Rob carries him. Coll is shot and killed (CONFRONTATION/ REVERSAL). As Alasdair dies he tells Rob about Mary's rape (REVERSAL). Rob captures a sol-dier's horse but it is shot and he is captured (REVERSAL). Rob is roped and dragged behind Cunningham's mount towards a meeting with Montrose at the Bridge of Orchy

(REVERSAL). Cunningham mocks him about having taken
his wife's honour (CONFRONTATION). Meanwhile Mary
visits Argyll and tells him that Rob would not betray him.
Montrose waits at the Bridge of Glen Orchy to see Mac-
Gregor brought to him 'broken but not dead'. He questions
Rob (CONFRONTATION) and orders him to be hung from
the bridge. In a dramatic escape (REVERSAL), Rob winds the
rope that has bound him around Cunningham's neck and
jumps from the bridge. The soldiers have to cut Rob free
to save Cunningham from being strangled (OPPOSITION/
REVERSAL). Rob escapes downstream, hiding inside the
rotting corpse of a cow (REVERSAL).

Meanwhile Mary and her sons move to yet another cottage, this time under Argyll's protection (REVERSAL), while
Cunningham and the soldiers move through Rob's lands,
killing his people and burning his villages (OPPOSITION).
Rob returns to Mary during the night and tells her he knows
of the rape. He confesses he was too proud (REVERSAL) but
she says he was right: he had to defend his honour. She tells
him she is pregnant and she does not know who is the father.
Rob accepts this (REVERSAL).

Rob goes to Argyll and asks him to arrange a duel between himself and Cunningham. Mary binds Rob's wounds
in preparation for the duel: it's clear that he has not yet recovered. Rob tells his sons that Mary is pregnant. He bids
Mary farewell and leaves to go to the duel. Argyll warns Rob
about Cunningham's prowess. Cunningham and Montrose
are waiting at the duelling-place when Argyll and Rob arrive
(CONFRONTATION). As Rob prepares to fight Cunningham
notices him wince from his wounds, telling him that Rob is
weakened. Argyll strikes a wager with Montrose: if Rob lives
Montrose will let him off with all his debts, and if he loses
Argyll will pay them off himself (CONFRONTATION). Rob
and Cunningham agree that there will be no quarter. Rob is
armed with a claymore, Cunningham with a rapier. As the
fight starts it's clear that Cunningham has the measure of
Rob Roy (OPPOSITION/CONFRONTATION). Cunningham
draws first blood. He has the edge on Rob in every way. Rob
seems slow, ponderous and ox-like by comparison with his

speed and agility. As Rob's strength ebbs Cunningham's confidence grows. He toys with Rob, wounding him several times (OPPOSITION/ CONFRONTATION). Eventually Rob is so weak he can hardly lift his sword. He is wounded once more and lets his sword drop. Cunningham seems to have won: he has Rob on his knees, his blade against his throat. He looks at Montrose, who nods. But as Cunningham gets ready to finish Rob off, Rob grabs the tip of Cunningham's sword. As Cunningham struggles to pull his blade free Rob retrieves his sword, stands and kills Cunningham with a single blow of his blade, cutting him from neck to breast bone (REVERSAL). Rob has fooled Cunningham from the start of the duel (REVERSAL).

Argyll tells Montrose he will hold him to the bargain. Montrose approaches Cunningham's corpse and looks down on his fallen champion without emotion. He kneels and takes from the corpse the picture of Cunningham's mother, revealing that he is Cunningham's real father (REVERSAL). Rob tells Argyll that he is returning home to Mary and that he will not fight any more duels (REVERSAL).

Act 2 ends at this point: there have been many confrontations, oppositions and reversals in Rob Roy's journey. His quest to escape Montrose and take revenge on Cunningham has taken him through loss and pain and brought him close to death; now he must return to the ordinary world and resume his life as best he can.

Act Three
Mary sits by her new cottage with her sons playing in the background (RESTORATION). Rob appears over the brae (RESOLUTION). He sees his home before him and breathes a sigh of gratitude. Mary and the boys see him. They run towards each other (RESTORATION). The last shot of the film shows the cottage in its beautiful glen. The story has been resolved, a different way of life restored. A new world has been made and this story can end, or another one begin.

8. *ROB ROY*: GENRE

Genre is vital to the film industry in that it sells a movie in advance to an audience.[29] A film is advertised through publicity such as posters, trailers and merchandising. The clearer its genre, the more likely it is to attract viewers. Audiences choose what they want to see because of their expectations of a film as well as liking a particular star or director. And different genres appeal to different audiences for many reasons: gender, age, social background, nationality and many other factors to do with personal and social identity all play a part in determining what a particular person will decide to spend money on in the cinema.

But genre is also complex and constantly evolves to reflect changing tastes and fashions. It can be a way too in which filmmakers and audiences push at the edges of what they know and like. Defining the genre of a film is not simple, and genres are not fixed. Very often a filmmaker will attempt to merge or cross two genres in order to make something new, and also to surprise and entertain the audience, who want to see something new as well as what they expect. This happens in *Rob Roy* – genre is respected and even loved, but it is also experimented with, and something original and unique is made.

Rob Roy: a consciously 'Hollywood' picture

Rob Roy was made in a consciously traditional way.[30] It looked not to European cinema, experimental film or the British tradition of small-scale, low-budget films concerned with social realism or crime, but to the traditional Hollywood style of making movies.

The Hollywood influence can be seen in the large-scale, sweeping music, the stellar cast, the romantic set pieces and crowd scenes, the action (stunts and exciting chases), the duelling and fight scenes (especially the swordfight at the climax of the film), the classic film structure, and the big (and usually masculine) themes of honour, courage and betrayal. Hollywood costume dramas of the 1930s and 40s developed a grand, melodramatic style that featured romance, swashbuckling action, lush cinematography and stirring music. The copperplate script on the caption at the start of *Rob Roy* deliberately imitates 'historical background' inserts in this type of rather old-fashioned movie.

One sub-genre of this family of films was the Scottish one, which lent itself naturally to this sort of treatment for the simple reason that the creator of the historical romance was Walter Scott, whose most famous stories were imitated by many other writers, creating a genre that passed into film.[31]

There are arguments for considering the Scottish historical film as part of the 'Heritage' genre. Heritage movies are controversial because many critics consider them backward looking and sentimental, a longing for the past, often an imperial one, using a large cast of famous actors and usually set in stately homes. They have been criticised for their concentration on sentiment and period detail at the expense of serious drama. Scottish pictures like *Brigadoon* and Disney's *Highland Rogue* no doubt fall into this category – they are fantasies that use Scotland as a backdrop rather than saying anything about the reality. *Rob Roy* also looks back at history and seems to say that a better time, the one represented by Highland culture, has passed. But against this argument is the 1995 film's concern for some historical accuracy, its graphic depiction of violence and its comment on traditional gender roles.

So perhaps we can say that some aspects of *Rob Roy* can be linked with the Hollywood costume drama and with the so-called Heritage genre, but that other important aspects of the movie are very different from them.

Rob Roy as a Western

As has already been said, Alan Sharp made his name in Hollywood by penning the screenplays for America's best-known genre, the Western. The Western was one of the first film genres and is at the heart not just of American cinema but also its culture. Thousands of cowboy movies have been made since the start of the film industry, and although the genre is often accused of being redundant, it has proved extremely resilient, with new ones still being made.[32]

The Western has depicted many different types of America, and its influence has extended far beyond the USA because of the power of the American film industry. There have been Spanish, Italian, Japanese and Indian Westerns, either set in the mythical American West or inventing these other countries' cultural equivalents. The 'spaghetti Westerns' of the Italian Sergio Leone, *A Fistful of Dollars* and *For a Few Dollars More* (filmed in Spain) and the Japanese director Kurosawa's *The Seven Samurai* (influenced by the Western *Shane*, and the inspiration for *The Magnificent Seven*) are examples of this.

The Western has shown itself capable of adapting to new ideas. Originally an expression of the triumph of American culture over the Native American one, with the 'Indians' represented as savage and hostile antagonists and the cowboys or settlers as peace-loving bringers of civilisation, it has changed this pattern more than once to reflect the changing politics and ideas of the time. In the sixties and seventies, with the Vietnam War and civil unrest making many Americans question their accepted definitions of right and wrong, Westerns began to cast the Native Americans and the incoming settlers in a very different light. The Native American tribes were portrayed much more sympathetically, and the incoming settlers as far from peaceful.

In *Rob Roy* the Highlanders are deliberately made to seem similar to Native Americans. The opening establishing shot shows the Highlanders as a people existing in their own setting, at ease in this landscape, skilfully tracking another group through the heather. MacDonald lifts a piece of cattle dung, sniffs it and bites it. He can tell exactly how long ago the beasts passed by. Similar tracking scenes can be seen in a hundred cowboy films. The drums and the wailing mouth-voice music in this scene are also reminiscent of the American West. The soundtrack is pounding and dramatic: it suggests wildness and exoticism but also a kind of civilisation, a different one from ours, with its own beliefs, laws and customs.

Other similarities between the Highlanders in *Rob Roy* and Native Americans in Westerns are the way the clansmen use animal noises and whistles to communicate when tracking. MacDonald does it to attract Rob's attention in the opening scene, and Rob does it when he and his followers are watching the sacking of the Highland village. This method of communicating in the field can be seen in many cowboy movies. It echoes the sort of warfare conducted against the settlers. Lacking firepower, often armed only with arrows and tomahawks, the 'Indians' are nonetheless effective because they never meet their opponents in open battle, but conduct a guerrilla war of stalking, ambush and swift retreats. This is exactly how Rob wages war against Montrose, knowing it is the best way to hurt him despite the protests of hotheads like Alasdair Roy. Coll, a wise old warrior, knows Rob is right and supports what he says at the meeting of the Gregorach. When the Highlanders are drawn into open battle, as when Alasdair Roy shoots at the soldiers, the superiority of the troops in direct conflict – their horses, muskets and discipline – immediately shows. Coll and Alasdair are killed and Rob is captured. This is exactly the type of uneven warfare shown in Westerns.

The Highlanders use the natural world around them to live. Their closeness to their landscape and the way their culture respects it is emphasised. When the troops chase them they know that they can disappear into the mist. They can sleep in the open: 'Lying wet-arsed in the heather,' Rob calls it. It is uncomfortable but not unusual for them.[33] They do it even when tracking. They can survive for long periods without shelter, as Rob does when he is forced to take to the hills after he has spurned Montrose. The Highlanders are almost impossible to catch in this wild landscape, even when pursued by trained troops. They live in small settlements and protect each other, sharing their resources among the community and trying to provide for the weak (contrast this with the huge, formal gardens of Montrose with their 'gelded trees', all of which belong to just one man). The clansfolk live in the midst of magnificent scenery. Mary and Rob share a lonely cottage by the loch-shore, using the resources around them, as shown when Rob washes in the loch after returning from tracking the castle-thieves led by Tam Sibbald, and

when Mary relieves herself by the shore. It is a portrait that
gives the lie to the Lowland idea of Highland clan culture
as primitive and crude. In fact, it is more democratic (shown
in the meeting of the Gregorach), more equal (the clans share
the land where Montrose seeks to own it outright), more honourable (expecting certain rules of combat to be observed),
more respectful and protective towards the vulnerable (the
old and the young in the clan) and, in the end, more adapt-
able than the Lowland one. Lowland culture, based on the
power of commerce, sees itself as superior to the Highland
one, which it seeks to exploit. 'I hear tell in America of noble
savages with paint on their faces and skins on their backs.
You'll be at home among them,' Killearn says sarcastically to
MacDonald. Killearn means it as an insult, but in the context of the film as a Western his remark points directly to the
comparison being made.

In many ways this depiction is linked particularly with one
era of the Western. The violence inflicted on Mary as Rob's
home is burned resembles the brutality against the North
American tribes shown in Westerns of the seventies – especially *Ulzana's Raid, Soldier Blue* and *Little Big Man*. This
kind of film expressed concern over American involvement
in Vietnam, where the US role was anything but heroic. In
particular, the My Lai Massacre in 1968 where over five hundred unarmed Vietnamese, mostly women and children, were
slaughtered by rampaging American troops – an incident
which only emerged after a cover-up by the army – brought
home to the average American the fact that their own soldiers
were capable of behaving brutally. Writers, filmmakers and
intellectuals began to express their disgust with the war
and demand that the troops be brought home. There was increasing questioning of America's past in books like *Bury My
Heart at Wounded Knee*, a history of the West seen from a
Native American point of view, which culminates in another
massacre perpetrated by US soldiers, in this case against the
Lakota people in 1890. And American Westerns began to de-
pict the white settlers as the aggressors against the indigenous
peoples of the West, forcing them from their land, cheating
them of their possessions and destroying their civilisation.

It is from this tradition of the Western that *Rob Roy* springs. 'Oh, you're a warrior, Archie, and no mistake,' Killearn says admiringly to Cunningham when the latter comes out of the cottage after raping Mary, but we the audience do not admire either man. The depiction of the violent attack has not been gratuitous, but makes a serious point: war is destructive, vicious and personal.

It should be added that Sharp and the film's director and producer also show a great love of the traditional Hollywood cowboy picture, acknowledging and using its uncanny ability to move with the times and adapt not just to different times but to different settings and cultures.

Many other scenes in the film, from the meeting of the Gregorach at the campfire to the fight with Tam Sibbald, also echo Westerns. The scene in the tavern where Rob confronts Killearn and kills Guthrie is a classic Western revenge-moment. It deliberately mimics the shootout: the unsheathing of weapons as the two men measure each other up, the rising tension, the moment of fear, the sudden burst of fatal action – all these elements can be found in Westerns.

9. *ROB ROY*: THEMES

Paternity

The theme of fatherhood or parenthood runs throughout the film. There are many instances of good and bad fathers and fatherly responsibility or the lack of it. The choices fathers make is a thread running through the whole story. On the one hand, Montrose's lack of any relationship with his natural son, Cunningham, shows the devastating effect of illegitimacy when it is not acknowledged. On the other, Rob and Mary's attitude towards the child possibly conceived during Mary's rape demonstrates how kindness and human love can conquer any stigma.

Although we don't know (or suspect) that Montrose is Cunningham's real father until the end of the film, there is certainly a similarity between them. They are physically alike and also alike in their personality. Both are ruthless, greedy and will go to any lengths to get what they want. 'You have a rare grasp of the conspirator's mind, Archibald. You are to be commended on it,' Montrose says to Cunningham, perhaps seeing something of himself in his son. Montrose should know: he is the arch-conspirator, ruthless in his dealings with his dependants, self-seeking and treacherous. On another occasion, having just spoken with Cunningham, Montrose says to Rob, 'I knew your father. An able man if not a wise one.' It is as if the idea of fatherhood has stayed with him after talking to Cunningham.

But Montrose never acknowledges Cunningham and it is clear that Cunningham has no idea who his real father is. Montrose keeps Cunningham as a lowly servant, hiding their real relationship from him, ensuring that he cannot leave because of his poverty and preventing him from seeking employment elsewhere. 'Your mother did not send you to me to debauch innocent girls,' he tells Cunningham, revealing his hypocrisy, as that is exactly what he did to Cunningham's mother. And he is outraged when Cunningham pretends to be 'a member of his household' rather than his guest, in order to run up bills with his tailor.

The harshness with which illegitimate children and the women who bear them are treated in Lowland society is made obvious in the film. Cunningham, a bastard himself, makes Betty pregnant, then like his own father disowns responsibility, forcing Betty into poverty when she loses her job. In despair, she kills herself. The cruelty towards fatherless children and unmarried women continues down the generations.

As an illegitimate son without 'a name' (meaning without any claim to social respectability), Cunningham is destitute, without status, forced to sell his only skill, his superb swordsmanship, to whoever will hire it. He has been forced into a lethal and lowly profession through accident of birth. 'You think me a gentleman because I have linen and can manage a lisp?' he asks Betty. He knows that a gentleman is something he can never become. It is clear that Cunningham's viciousness and sadistic delight in inflicting pain stem from his frustration at being 'without honour'.

The way Rob Roy and Mary treat the child who might have been conceived from the rape is completely different. 'Rob would be hard pressed to love such a bastard, would he not? ...It is a wise father knows his own child.' Killearn says to Mary as he tries to bluster his way out of captivity. But he underestimates Mary, Rob and Highland culture, and his stupidity in assuming that Mary will be intimidated brings about his own death. The rape and the unborn child are matters of shame, especially to hotheads like Alasdair Roy, but Mary hides them not just because of dishonour but also out of fear at how Rob will react. Cunningham's action has been to provoke Rob to open warfare, and Mary knows it. She keeps her pregnancy a secret to protect her husband, not because she is so ashamed that she will never tell him. She almost tells Rob after Killearn has been killed, but it is the wrong moment. When Rob returns exhausted and wounded to the cottage Argyll has provided after escaping from Montrose's troops, he has learned the truth. 'You should have told me, Mary,' he says, but with sadness, not anger. 'O husband, I could not,' Mary answers. When she goes on to say she is pregnant Rob's first thought is for her, not for what other people will think. Next day he tells his sons there is another baby on the way. The child – ironically the offspring of Rob's

worst enemy – will be raised as part of the family and the
stigma of illegitimacy will be prevented. There will be a happy and healthy home life, and the cycle of shame and neglect,
passed from Montrose to Cunningham and from Cunningham to his own unborn child, will be broken.

In this important sense, Rob is shown to be far stronger
and more enduring than Montrose, Cunningham and all his
enemies, and Highland culture as represented by the family
shown at the end of the film is shown to be much more adapt-
able, loving and caring than the supposedly more civilised
society that threatens it. It can absorb illegitimacy, and possibly much more. It is a note of optimism and hope for the
future.

'I have his child inside me, and I would fain have a father
for him,' Mary tells Argyll while asking for his protection.
It should also be remembered that Alan Sharp was illegitimate and adopted himself. Mary gets what she wants in the
end, and the last shot of the remote croft tells us that she,
Rob and their family will live out their days in peace.

Honour

Honour is one of the most important themes in the film, and
is referred to again and again, especially by Rob. (In the caption that opens the film, 'honour' is the last word on the card,
ensuring that that the audience will remember it as the action starts.)

At the Standing Stones, after returning from the raid
where he killed Tam Sibbald, Rob explains to his sons what
honour is. 'All men with honour are kings, but not all kings
have honour,' he says. It is a valuable thing but not even the
greatest are guaranteed it. 'Honour is what no man can give
you and no man can take away,' he adds, and 'Women are the
heart of honour ... It grows in you and speaks to you.'

This code is the one Rob lives by. By implication it is observed right across the Highlands. When tracking the cattle
Rob offers Tam Sibbald a deal: he can die now at Rob's hand
or on the gallows. Tam understands this: it will be an honourable end rather than a shameful and squalid one. He
attempts to fight thus ensuring his own death. As part of his

promise, Rob lets the other broken men and the woman who follows them leave without further harm.

Honour is above social status. It cannot be taken away or conferred: it has to be earned. Rob shows us that he bases his whole life on this idea when he offers his oath as security for the borrowed money. 'When my word is given it is good,' he tells Montrose, ignoring the fact that the Marquis is much more interested in his land than any promises. He still relies on this honourable agreement between men when he returns to Montrose to ask for more money after the first loan has been stolen:

> Montrose: You signed a paper.
> Rob Roy: And I will honour it.
> Montrose: Oh, ply me not with your honour, man.

And it is for honour's sake, the importance of his word, that Rob refuses to repay Montrose by saying Argyll is a Jacobite. He is prepared to sacrifice his lands, his possessions and his freedom rather than break his word.

The Lowlanders, when they mention honour at all, do it contemptuously. 'You honour me, James, to serve me with your own hand,' Montrose spits at Argyll when the latter upbraids him. The Lowlanders and landowners live by quite a different code. Profit is their motive. 'Wolves at lambing,' are Rob's words for them. But even early in the film it is apparent that the Highland code of honour, while admirable, is powerless in the face of this greed. Indeed, at points it seems almost wilfully ignorant of the inevitable results of its own inability to change. Rob takes to the hills believing that Mary and his house will be safe from Montrose, that the code of honour will be observed. Montrose immediately instructs Cunningham to bring Rob back 'broken but not dead,' and Cunningham's first act is to attack and destroy Rob's home. Rob has been wrong to assume that the 'rules of war' will be observed. When Cunningham rapes Mary he 'takes her honour' as a deliberate insult to Rob. Mary knows that Rob's sense of honour is his weak spot, and she protects him from taking rash revenge by hiding the attack from him.

But equally, the Lowland contempt for honour and high regard for money is also inadequate. It devalues all it comes into contact with. It reduces the Highlanders to rootless dependants and seems at first to win the battle against Rob, forcing him from his lands, his wife, his family and his place in society. It can rely on the services of desperate men like Guthrie to do its dirty work and betray Rob. But not even the master-bargainer Killearn can exploit his way out of every situation. His money fails to protect him from Rob's fury in the tavern. He tries to talk his way out of Rob's custody after he has been captured, only to be faced with something he can't buy: Rob's desperation and anger. 'I'm past caring, Killearn,' Rob tells him, and Killearn is silent, knowing he has nothing to offer. Most fatal of all is his inability to recognise Mary's outrage when he tries to blackmail her by telling Rob of the pregnancy. He fails to see that not everything has a price and can be bought and sold like a commodity, and pays with his life.

'This point of honour might likely kill you, sir,' Argyll says to Rob when the Highlander proposes the duel with Cunningham. The duke knows that honour is not enough when dealing with vicious men like Montrose and Cunningham. But what Argyll does not know is that by this point in the film Rob has changed. He has realised that honour can never win when your enemy does not play by the rules. He confesses to Mary that he has been too proud. Sharp the screenwriter skilfully builds the audience's fear that, as Argyll expects, Rob will be brought low yet again. We expect the Highlander to fight by the rules and Cunningham to use cunning and surprise. 'You are here on a matter of honour. I am here to make sure you settle it honourably,' the referee says to both men as the duel starts. But the fight already seems unequal. How can honour win the day?

Change
After the credits end, and before the first shot of the film, in true Hollywood fashion, comes a caption:
> **At the dawn of the 1700s, famine, disease and the greed of great Noblemen were changing Scotland forever.**

> With many emigrating to the Americas, the
> centuries-old Clan system was slowly being
> extinguished.
> This story symbolizes the attempt of the indi-
> vidual to withstand these processes and, even in
> defeat, retain respect and honour.

Captions in traditional films state in large terms what the
audience is about to see. This caption does exactly that. It
states clearly that one of the key themes of the story we are
about to see is change.

We see change in the famine and disease the elderly and
young Highlanders are suffering in Rob's lands. We see it
in the 'broken men' who are appearing in greater numbers
across the Highlands, as Rob tells Mary. The fact that the
outlaw Tam Sibbald once played football with Rob at Crieff
market shows us that many in the Highlands are being
forced into crime, and that a disastrous social change is taking place. Other figures such as Will Guthrie and Betty, and
their fates, contribute to this picture. Guthrie is a broken
man after his defeat by Cunningham, dismissed from Argyll's employment, prepared to do anything to make money,
even to be disloyal to another Highlander. Betty is destitute
in a poor society, with nowhere to turn after her dismissal
by Montrose. They are both desperate figures and both lose
their lives.

The greed of the noblemen, and the way they are forcing
change on Highland society,[34] is seen in Montrose's exploitation of the clansfolk. Killearn, his factor, is employed to
extend his master's profits, and makes his own on the side.
Argyll too is another of the 'wolves at lambing'. When it comes
to money and profit, the noblemen and the Lowlanders are
all the same.

The centuries-old clan system, which is now disintegrat-
ing,[35] is seen at the meeting of the Gregorach when Rob has
to persuade them to his point of view. He is not a tyrant but
someone who leads because of the respect people have for
his skills. MacDonald explains to Killearn when he waits
for the money that nobody in Highland society is a 'Master'

and nobody a slave or servant. By contrast, Lowland society is full of servants, and even slaves, as the presence of the black boy who constantly attends Montrose shows. But the Highlanders are being turned into servants by the landowners, who either employ them or evict them from their homes. Money is something the Highlanders do not have and know little about: they are naïve with cash. The move from a bartering system to one based on currency is also part of social change. The clansman MacDonald, who is due to emigrate, illustrates another aspect of social upheaval: the drain of people to America.[36] More and more people are leaving the Highlands because of the pressure of increasing poverty. As MacDonald passes the sign for Greenock we wonder whether he will be tempted to leave there and then. Plenty of other people have left for America from there before.

As Cunningham pursues Rob, we witness the beginnings of the annihilation of Highland society. The MacGregors are unable to defend themselves against Cunningham's ruthlessness and Montrose's well-trained troops. The men are killed and their families are driven from their homes. Rob eventually triumphs over Cunningham but, tellingly, the social change outlined at the start of the film continues. The last shot tells us that Rob will take no further part in politics, war and the affairs of great men, but it is just one ending, the conclusion of an individual story. The landowners will continue to steal the Highlanders' land, girls like Betty will continue to suffer, and other greedy factors will come. Rob's personal survival has ultimately depended on his ability to meet this change, to redefine his notion of honour and to turn from the big world of conflict to the small world of the domestic.

One way in which a narrative enacts its key messages is to invent characters who stand for or embody different sides of a conflict. *Rob Roy* does this superbly well, allowing the characters involved to retain their convincing individuality and authenticity. Rob represents Highland society. He is heroic and adventurous, bold, honourable and caring, a true leader. But he is more than a little out-dated, and vulnerable to his enemies. This is not wholly a flaw – he has not caused the conflict with his greedier opponents – but it is partly. His stiff-necked refusal to budge from his ideals leads him to betray those he most loves. It may not be a major fault but it is one that causes him and Mary great pain. It is also one he can learn from. At the end of the duel, when Rob grabs Cunningham's sword with his hand, he shows that his concept of honour has changed, and that he is prepared break the rules of the game. And so he survives. The film's message seems to be that Highland culture, so reduced during the eighteenth, nineteenth and twentieth centuries, nevertheless might have a chance of survival today if it proves as resilient.

Rob's opponents can also be read as symbolic of the forces involved in the battle over the Highlands. Montrose can be seen as power, Cunningham as violence, and Killearn as commerce. Together these three stop at nothing to get what they want. They are governed by no code of honour or moral behaviour and nothing is strong enough to oppose them. Interestingly, these same forces are present in Walter Scott's original novel, although they are presented very differently, and as the spirits of necessary, if not altogether welcome, change. The Hanoverian government, its troops occupying the Highlands, and the character of Baillie Nicol Jarvie are the novel's equivalents. It is in the figures of Jarvie/Killearn that the difference between Scott's novel and Sharp's screenplay is most clear. In the first, commerce is seen as the spirit of the age, the new fashion which will bring great benefits and wealth to the newly created nation of Britain. (Indeed in many ways the Baillie is the real hero of Scott's novel, the one likely to triumph, unlike the Highland leader Rob Roy.) In the second, commerce, personified by Killearn, is cold, calculating, greedy, exploitative and ultimately futile.

Similarly, Mary stands not just as an individual but also as the often under-represented figure of Highland women. Her courage, determination and loyalty are qualities that Sharp presents as admirable, things to aspire to in life. (She is also similar in this respect to Helen MacGregor, Rob Roy's wife in Walter Scott's novel.) Betty can be seen to personify younger women who are exploited in this society, while Guthrie, Alasdair Roy, Coll and Tam Sibbald also stand for

types as well as being convincing in their own right. They
are *archetypes*: larger than individuals, but not stereotypes
– a device often used in film. Through them, the film's main
themes – honour, betrayal, change and the disintegration of
a way of life – are played out on the surface of the movie, its
narrative.[37]

Swordfight: Point versus Edge
The swordfight in *Rob Roy* is justly famous. It was praised
by critics and provides an exciting, gripping climax to the
story.

A swordfight is one of the tropes of the swashbuckler sub-
genre, which has links to the costume drama and the Heritage genres. Swordfights also appear in the *Star Wars* series,
which is arguably a science fiction version of the swashbuckler sub-genre. Swashbucklers were long out of fashion when
Rob Roy was made, although they have since made a spectacular return with Disney's *Pirates of the Caribbean* series.

Swordfights in traditional swashbucklers tended to rely
for effect on the speed and agility of the contestants. They
were real fencing matches fought with rapiers – long flexible
pointed blades – where the audience would be caught up in
the spectacle of fast action and physical prowess.

But the swordfight in *Rob Roy* differs from these versions.
It is linked to another theme in the film, that of the old versus the new in Highland culture. Two contrasting styles of
weapon and fighting are shown; they stand for the cultures
represented by the fighters; and the outcome of the fight is
not what seems likely. The fight is played slowly, with many
pauses and sudden bursts of action. Rather than the swift-
ness of the action or the sword skill of the combatants, the
emotions of the two opponents are the focus of the action. In
fact, the entire sequence (meaning the series of shots that
show the fight from beginning to end) resembles a gunfight
in a Western much more than a swashbuckler duel.

The swordfight is worth looking at in some detail because
it says much about this theme, and this can be best done
by examining the contrast between the swords themselves:
point versus edge.

The claymore, which Rob chooses as his weapon, is the traditional sword of the clansmen. It has appeared in the film during the first duel between Cunningham and Guthrie. Cunningham makes his contempt for it clear: 'If I had to kill an ox, a claymore would be my first choice.' This is an insult to Will Guthrie and to the Highland method of fighting, comparing it to little more than butchery. But it is also true, as becomes obvious when Cunningham easily beats Argyll's champion. (Guthrie's cowardly and boastful nature is confirmed when he attempts to stab Cunningham in the back after the duel, and also when he offers his services as a tracker to Montrose through Killearn, only to be killed by Rob Roy in the tavern.)

Cunningham's weapon, the rapier, is much more sophisticated. Instead of the hacking edge, it uses the stabbing point. It resembles Cunningham himself: thinner and seemingly weaker than what it opposes, but in reality much more deadly. Handled by an expert like Cunningham, who uses subtlety and finesse as well as strength and speed, it will always defeat the heavier sword. As the fighter with the claymore becomes worn down by its weight, the rapier will inevitably win, and this is exactly what seems to happen during the duel between Cunningham and Rob.

Point, as personified by Cunningham, is mocked by the Highlanders when they first see him prepare for a contest. To them his actions seem showy and affected, and so does his weapon. Point represents the new, the threat to the established way of things in Highland culture from outside. Edge represents the old, what the clansmen know and are used to, and what they wish to preserve.

Cunningham proves himself more than a match for Guthrie; he is also an expert soldier, bringing a new ruthlessness to war and conquest. Point seems invulnerable. By contrast, edge seems outdated, cumbersome and clumsy, as Rob finds himself, for all his skills, constantly on the defensive, and usually outwitted. Edge expects a set of rules to be followed, which point simply ignores.

The contrast between the blades comes to its climax during the second duel in the film. Cunningham's deadly expertise is well known by now. Argyll warns Rob that he stands little chance of winning. Rob's chances seem even less because he is still weak from his wounds. As the two men prepare to fight, testing out their different weapons, Cunningham notices Rob wince – a clear sign that he can be beaten. As the men face each other, Rob seems the one full of anger and the need for revenge, which was what Cunningham wanted. It is Rob who first says, 'No quarter will be asked.' Rob's emotions seem to be ruling his head.

As the fight begins, point seems to have all the advantages. Cunningham is smaller, more mobile and agile. He pulls off his wig to make himself even lighter. He takes advantage of Rob's wounds to make his attacks. Within a few strokes it is clear that point is superior. Rob defends himself as best he can but is wounded across the stomach. Cunningham holds his rapier point out and dominates the middle of the space, while Rob holds his claymore in defence. Cunningham wounds Rob a second time on the arm. When Rob does attack he exhausts himself. He looks increasingly slow and despairing. He has to use both hands to hold up his heavy sword, a sure sign that he is weakening. Now all he can do is back away from the point. He is wounded again across the other arm. At last he can only drag his sword-tip across the floor. With Rob's last attack, Cunningham wounds him deeply in the stomach, making Rob drop his claymore and fall to his knees. Cunningham knows he has won. He raises Rob's head with his sword-point just as he did with Guthrie in the first duel. This time the loser will pay with his life. Point seems to have completely defeated edge.

What happens next is one of the film's key moments, and a complete reversal of what the audience has been led to expect. As Cunningham gloatingly looks towards Montrose, the apparently defeated Highlander grabs the point of the rapier with his hand and holds onto it. As Cunningham tries to free his blade Rob retrieves his claymore, rises with a roar and delivers a deadly blow, almost cutting Cunningham in half. Rob studies his wounded hand and walks past Cunningham's bloody corpse, dropping his claymore as he goes. The deadly efficiency of the outsider, the apparently unconquerable precision of the rapier, has been despatched by a single hacking stroke. Edge has defeated point after all.

Rob has fooled Cunningham and Montrose. Knowing he stood no chance in an equal contest, he has pretended to fight to the limits of his strength so as to have the opportunity to deliver the fatal blow. He has deliberately allowed Cunningham to see that he is weak and has allowed himself to be wounded. Rob has also broken the rules of the duel. He has cheated by grabbing the tip of Cunningham's blade, the last thing Cunningham – and the audience – expected of him.

The dropping of the claymore by Cunningham's body, and Rob's return to his family in the film's closing scene, also tell us that Rob will never fight again. The old ways represented by the claymore are gone, but Rob and Highland culture have proved themselves capable of change, and the film ends.

10. *ROB ROY*: CHARACTERS

Rob Roy: 'Honour is a gift a man gives himself.'
Rob Roy is the hero of the film, the centre of the action and narrative, and the film's protagonist. He is the victim of the plot to steal the money and Montrose's duplicity, and from that moment is a man on the run. His quest is first to escape, then to protect his family and people, and finally to take his revenge on Cunningham.

Rob is a great warrior and a wise leader. He easily defeats Tam Sibbald and even offers him mercy in killing him on the spot rather than leading him to the gallows. He also defeats and kills Argyll's champion Will Guthrie. He excels in any fight, showing himself quicker, stronger and more astute than any opponent, even his greatest foe, Cunningham. Unlike Cunningham, Rob takes no pleasure in killing. He spares Will Guthrie when first challenged in the tavern by nicking his hand on Guthrie's blade, claiming that the spilt blood settles the matter. He is an expert tracker, leading his followers in the hunt for the stolen cattle. He is brave and imposing, going down to deal with Tam Sibbald alone when he could have attacked the robbers in the night. He is merciful, allowing the rest of the robbers to go free. He is well known and held in high regard, not just by his own clansmen but throughout the Highlands. He is tall, strong, virile and handsome, loving to his wife and affectionate to his family. He is kind, worrying about the condition of the weaker members of his clan after he returns to the township. He feels responsible for their condition and so risks taking the loan from Montrose. He is clever, outwitting Cunningham in the swordfight, using the right tactics against Montrose, and eventually being allowed to live out the rest of his life in peace with Mary, despite having being condemned, pursued and almost killed.

Rob shows that he will walk away from a fight rather than put other people in danger. He takes to the hills after refusing to condemn Argyll, thinking that Mary will be safe from Montrose's revenge (an act he later regrets). He advises the Gregorach not to attack Montrose directly. When he sees the cottages being burnt by Cunningham, he orders his followers not to fire because he knows they stand no chance against the troopers, and is proved right when Alasdair Roy gives their position away.

Rob is not the master of his people but someone they appoint. This is contrasted with Montrose's cold arrogance, his acute and fragile consciousness of his social position and his lack of respect for those he considers his social inferiors, such as the servant he contemptuously pushes aside as he stands over Cunningham's dead body.

Rob's main characteristic at the start of the story is honour. 'It was not done for Your Grace, but for his own honour, which he holds dearer than myself, his sons, his clan or kin, and for which I have oft chided him,' Mary tells Argyll when she goes to him to look for shelter, and to tell him of Montrose's treachery. Time and again Rob refers to honour. It is his touchstone on how to behave in all things: '...it is him and his way, and, were he other, he would not be Robert Roy MacGregor,' Mary says.

However, Rob's concern for honour, especially his own, is not without its blind side. There is a touch of pride in his refusal to see beyond it. His pride in his word, admirable though it might be, constantly leads him into making mistakes. He fails to prevent Killearn and Cunningham from cheating him out of his money and his land. He abandons his family in the belief that Montrose will not attack them. After kidnapping Killearn, he believes that he can try and punish the factor fairly and according to rules of war, instead of understanding the reality of the situation. He underestimates Cunningham's ruthlessness and pays for it with a narrow escape from death at Bridge of Orchy, and with the harm done to Mary.

Rob Roy's character changes as the film progresses. Like many protagonists in adventure films, he is tested beyond the limits of his strength and endurance. He is roped and dragged behind a horse after being captured by Cunningham. He is kicked in the face and tied like an animal. He is told he is going to be hung like a common criminal from the bridge. When he escapes down the burn, he has to hide inside the rotting belly of a cow, cutting his way into it with a horn and crawling through the intestines. He loses his lands, his family, his social position, his money, his friends, his brother, his strength and his pride and is reduced to hiding among stinking guts. The proud hero is reduced to a fugitive barely able to crawl from the fight. He is badly wounded, literally branded by his ordeal.

Rob confesses more than once during the film that he has been wrong. When the Gregorach meets, he says the injury done to him and Mary is 'far past what I had expected, even from such as Montrose.' (He does not yet know the true extent of the injury done to Mary). Returning to Mary after his dramatic escape, he says that he should have 'packed his pride and given Montrose his way' – for if he had, Mary would not have been violated and Coll and Alasdair Roy would still be alive. Mary defends him from his self-disgust, but by the end of the film Rob has changed. He wins the duel against Cunningham by being prepared to cheat, and so gains his revenge, his safety, and his reunion with his family. His family and domestic life are now more important to him than honour.

Cleaning his wounds after his last battle, Rob laughs when Argyll proposes more matches and says, 'I hope Your Grace will live so long.' The last shots showing Rob's reunion with his family need no dialogue because the action tells us that Rob will stand on his honour no more. The closing scene as the credits come up shows us where he will live peacefully for the rest of his life.

Liam Neeson is one of Northern Ireland and Hollywood's greatest stars, often playing the romantic lead or the action hero. He appeared in supporting roles in major movies early in his career, such as *The Mission* (1986), and in leading roles on smaller budget films such as *Lamb* (1986) and *The Big Man* (1990). He went on to appear in lead roles in major Hollywood productions, most notably *Schindler's List* (1993). After *Rob Roy*, he continued to appear in lead or supporting roles in major productions such as *Star Wars: The Phantom Menace* (1999), and *Gangs of New York* (2002).

Mary MacGregor: 'To stay home with your wife and children instead of taking to the hills like a fox.'

Mary, Rob's wife, plays a significant role in the film. She is a strong and forceful personality in her own right and, although she keeps house and looks after her children while Rob is in hiding, she shows she has the courage to face anything, even him. She argues with him when he decides to leave, accusing him of walking away from what he should defend, and she is proved right. She is more than loyal to Rob: she is deeply in love with him, and he with her. She protects Rob by hiding the fact that she has been raped from him. She also supports him when he despairs, successfully persuades Argyll to offer her and her family a new cottage, and, even when Rob leaves again to fight Cunningham in the duel, understands and accepts his reasons.

The atrocity at Inversnaid is one of the most powerful and striking scenes in the film: it shows the brutal violence of war as it really is. Rape is shown as a weapon of war, a calculated act of brutality against women, its intention being to terrorise its victims. Cunningham's motive is to do just that to Mary, and to insult Rob's sense of honour and so draw him into open battle. He would have succeeded if he really had crushed Mary's spirit. But after the rape the depth of Mary's courage is shown. She walks from the house where others would perhaps have rather burnt to death than face Killearn's and the soldiers' mockery. Cunningham guesses this: 'She'll be out. She's a hater, that one.' She endures Killearn's taunts and Alasdair Roy's horror and shame. She continues to endure them as Rob speaks at the meeting of the Gregorach. 'Rob is right. What cannot be helped must be endured.' Her words have an ironic ring because the audience knows what Mary must endure, while Rob does not. Mary's refusal to tell Rob is made more understandable when Killearn correctly guesses that she is pregnant. She is in a terrible dilemma. She cannot be sure that the unborn child is Rob's. The alternatives are to abort it or to tell her husband. She is in a similar predicament to Betty, who has killed herself rather than give birth to an illegitimate child.

Mary's characteristic is her great strength. She is as strong as Rob, perhaps more so. She faces trials as demanding and difficult as his. Violated, twice driven from her home, pregnant and looking after her older children, and offering

what support she can to outcasts like Betty, she nevertheless
survives and keeps her family together. Her spirit is indomi-
table. She can be contrasted with the cold fish Montrose, who
never allows his public mask to slip. She remains defiant even
at at her lowest moment. 'I will think of you dead until my
husband makes you so … and then I will think on you no more,'
she says to Cunningham after the rape. She is never subdued
and never gives in. She takes her revenge on Killearn when
he tries to bargain his way out of imprisonment, and eventually her words come true: her husband kills Cunningham,
who dies forgotten. Cunningham's own child will be integrated
into a loving Highland family and will never know who its
real father was, all because of Mary's courage. Although
Rob is the protagonist of the film, Mary is also heroic. Her
sacrifice and endurance are the equal of his, and she shows
greater wisdom.

Jessica Lange became a leading female star with *King
Kong* (1976). She remained at the forefront of American film
with *Frances* (1982), based on the life of actress Frances
Farmer, *Tootsie* (1982), and in major roles in the following decades in films such as *Cape Fear* (1991) and *Big Fish*
(2003). She has worked with most of Hollywood's leading
actors including Dustin Hoffman, Jack Nicholson and Robert
De Niro. She is famous for playing strong, independent women
who face difficulties with courage.

Cunningham: 'Broken but not dead. It has a ring to it.'
The character of Cunningham is one of the triumphs of the
film, and the only one that is almost entirely fictional. His
effectiveness as Rob Roy's opponent and his main characteristic of cold-hearted ruthlessness make him one of the most
memorable villains in British film. However, despite the
crimes we see him commit he also has a vulnerable side, a
fact that makes him seem human, and therefore real instead
of a one-dimensional monster.

Cunningham is a cold and deadly killer. The difference
between him and the rest of humanity is obvious from the
moment he first appears – a fop in this highly masculine
society, an Englishman mocked for his accent and background

in Scotland. But despite his flamboyant manners and appearance, he is a match for anyone. He beats Guthrie easily and proves himself the best swordsman in Scotland. He takes pleasure in killing people and inflicting pain, toying with his victims, as when he tracks MacDonald through the wood and impales him to the tree, making sure that the clansman knows he has taken the money before he dies. He cold-bloodedly destroys Rob's home and devastates the MacGregor lands.

Sharp makes it clear in the character of Cunningham that sadism and ruthlessness make good soldiers. Cunningham is an expert military man, taking his troops to the heart of MacGregor territory and subduing it. He is a match for Rob in strength and tactical awareness. He knows that, if he can anger Rob enough to make him fight openly, he will win. He out-manoeuvres Rob by attacking his homestead from the water instead of coming by road. (Alasdair Roy, who has fallen asleep and so fails to guard the shore, demonstrates the shortcomings of the untrained soldier, full of bravado but lacking vital discipline.) Cunningham also proves more ruthless than Rob expects. It is only when Rob fights his nemesis face to face that he proves his equal.

But this is only one side of Cunningham. The other is that he is keenly aware of his own lowly social position. 'I am but a bastard abroad,' he says to Betty. He doesn't know who his father is and doubts if his mother does either. He has no money and runs up huge debts with his tailor. His protector Montrose keeps him in thrall with this poverty. The stain of illegitimacy in eighteenth-century Scotland sinks deep. Cunningham will never be considered a gentleman: he will never be admitted to respectable society or be able to make much of himself. He is an outcast from social position, from honour, from his adopted country, and from anything to do with family and a home. (Contrast this with Rob Roy, who even at his lowest ebb has all these things.) Perhaps the hatred with which Cunningham destroys Rob's home is behind this. His mannerisms – the flamboyant bows and gestures he makes as he prepares to fight – are more like an exaggerated parody of gentility than the real thing, as if he can only ape them, or is mocking the society which has so completely excluded him. It is not surprising that he has a vicious side and that violence excites him.

At the end of the film, when Cunningham is killed in the duel, we can almost feel sorrow for him despite his crimes as Montrose takes from him the medallion showing his mother's portrait. Here is the secret behind Cunningham's cruelly wasted life: Montrose is his real father but Cunningham has died without ever knowing it. His viciousness has been created in him by his isolation and frustration. The fact that we can feel some sympathy for him despite having seen his violent acts is testament to the power and perception of Sharp's characterisation and Tim Roth's portrayal.

Tim Roth first came to public attention in *Made in Britain* (1982), where he played a violent skinhead. He went on to appear in major American films such as *Reservoir Dogs* (1992) and *Pulp Fiction* (1994). He is known for playing characters who are misfits and who do not fit the role they are forced or expected to play, often with violent results. He went on to appear in other major productions such as *Planet of the Apes* (2001) and *The Incredible Hulk* (2008). He was nominated for an Oscar for his performance in *Rob Roy*.

Killearn: 'Money, Archie – what else?'

Killearn's key characteristic is greed for money. He is concerned with cash above everything and is prepared to do anything for it. Practically every line spoken by him shows him reducing everything to its material worth. He knows the price of everything and the value of nothing, even the contents of a chamberpot: 'It's almost pure spirit or I'm no judge of a pint of piss'. His toast is 'Business – and profit!'

Killearn always goes too far to get what he wants. He is cowardly and manipulative. He never gets involved in any physical action himself but draws aside when it threatens, as when he tries to persuade Guthrie to defend him against Rob in the tavern. He is useful to Montrose as a means of increasing his wealth but is also disposable. Montrose is angered by Killearn's kidnap only because he sees it as an affront to himself. 'My factor will call upon Your Grace's factor,' the lords say to each other at the start and end of the film. The fact that Killearn is dead by the end makes no difference – there are plenty more like him and the system of commerce will continue.

Everything about Killearn has been fitted into that system. When we first see him, he is running through Montrose's gardens. He looks clumsy, awkward, obedient and unnatural. Underneath the ugly accoutrements (the wig, buckled shoes and the too-tight clothes) he is a man who has grown into an almost obscene shape, like the 'gelded trees' on Montrose's estate.

He is an informant, Montrose's eyes and ears, who brings him intelligence even when it is little more than rumour. He tells Montrose about Cunningham's debts and spreads the rumour that Rob Roy stole Montrose's cattle himself. He also reveals Betty's pregnancy, leading to her dismissal from her job in Montrose's house, and then to her suicide. He has nothing but contempt for the Highlanders and their old-fashioned ways of barter. He patronises them and talks down to them. 'Well that's a great comfort to us all, I must say, what with a thousand pounds at risk,' he says to Rob when they strike the deal at the tavern.

It is Killearn who first suggests the plot to steal the money to Cunningham, so breaking his position of trust with the people he is meant to be collecting money from. He cheats MacDonald at the tavern by lying about the Note of Credit and paying him in cash instead, which can never be replaced. He stands by and watches the atrocity at Rob's house at Inversnaid, which Mary finds even worse than taking part. To the end of his life, he thinks he can blackmail and exploit others. Imprisoned by Rob, he still tries to threaten Mary. Mary draws a knife and stabs him and Alasdair Roy finishes the job off by drowning him in the loch. His death, like his life, is ugly and, although Rob sees the killing as a mistake, no one mourns him.

Brian Cox is a Scottish actor who has appeared in many television series such as *Minder* (1982). His breakthrough came with his role in *Manhunter* (1986), where he played the original Hannibal Lecter. He has become a regular main supporting actor in television and British and American film productions such as *The Bourne Supremacy* (2004) and *The Flying Scotsman* (2006).

Montrose: 'I am James Graham, Marquis of Montrose, and I will not be mocked!'

The key characteristic of James Graham, Marquis of Montrose, is pride. He hides his greed for money and his fear under arrogance and consciousness of his high position. He surrounds himself with servants and sycophants like Killearn, whom he treats with disdain. He is cold and overbearing, conscious of his social standing above all other things: 'Remember your place, sir! That's all I ask of any man.' 'Damn his pride!' he says of Argyll when the Duke takes him to task for spreading rumours at court – but it is his own egotism which is hurt. He is incapable of kindness even towards his son, whom he keeps at a distance and treats like a chattel. 'Do not – do not, I say – speak in my stead.' He is acutely conscious of who he is and sees any criticism as an insult, something he will not tolerate. 'See to it that I am not mocked,' is his instruction to Cunningham and Killearn when Rob has been hunted from his lands. And, when Rob and the MacGregors strike back by thieving his cattle and kidnapping his factor, he feels he is being made a fool of, which drives him to greater fury. Rob has been right when he has guessed how to best get back at Montrose.

The Marquis is treacherous, constantly trying to undermine his rival Argyll at court in order to become the greatest man in Scotland. He is as quick as his factor to spot a possible profit, and just as capable of theft, but less open about it. His power allows him to exploit people on a larger scale. He upbraids Killearn for charging only one-fifth interest on the loan to Rob Roy until his factor reminds him that Rob has three hundred acres of land to use as security. Montrose knows that £1000 Scots is a paltry sum for this land, but pretends he cares only about the money as he makes the bargain with Rob. (Killearn knows that the land is what his master is really after, and that the theft of the money will go unpunished, provided the thieves cover their tracks.)

Montrose is also shrewd. Like all the aristocrats and Lowlanders shown in the film (Cunningham, Argyll, Montrose and Killearn) the ability to make money, drive a hard bargain and exploit other people is prized. 'Do you take me entirely for a Whig, sir?' he asks when Cunningham tries to pretend he has won money at gaming, angry that Cunningham might underestimate his ability to sniff out a profit. (The Whigs at this point of history were the political party associated with personal liberty and social reform.) He guesses that Killearn and Cunningham have had a hand in the disappearance of the money, as Killearn warns in the garden. He sees that Cunningham is 'in cash' from the finery he can suddenly afford to wear. 'I care not what you and that greasy capon have cooked up, but put an end to this impudence against me,' he tells him. He will use any information he has to get what he wants.

John Hurt is one of Britain's leading and most respected character actors, known for his versatility. In *10 Rillington Place* (1971) he played the part of Timothy Evans, who was wrongly hanged for the murder of his wife and child in 1950 in a famous miscarriage of justice; in *The Naked Civil Servant* (1975) he played the part of Quentin Crisp, a flamboyant homosexual; in *I, Claudius* (1976) the mad Emperor Caligula; and in *Midnight Express* (1978) he was the heroin addict Max. In *The Elephant Man* (1980) he took on the lead role of John Merrick. He was the unfortunate astronaut Kane out of whose stomach the monster burst in the first of the *Alien* films (1979). He also appeared in *Scandal* (1989) and *Harry Potter and the Philosopher's Stone* (2001). He often plays outcasts but has appeared in a huge number of different roles in his long and distinguished career.

Argyll

The Duke of Argyll is an older man, in reality Montrose's social superior but whose position at court can be threatened. The question of the succession, with the reigning Protestant monarch Anne about to die and the possibility of the return of the Catholic Stuart kings, makes even the greatest aristocrats vulnerable. Suspicion of supporting the Stuarts can put even a duke's head in a noose, and this is the situation Argyll finds himself in when Montrose starts to spread rumours.

Argyll has something of the Highland tradition of honour about him but is also a member of the ruling class. Rob includes him among the '...wolves at lambing': as greedy as the other landowners when there is profit to be made. When Mary comes to him to ask his protection from Montrose his first instinct is to say no: Rob's dispute with Montrose is nothing to do with him. It is only when she goes on to say that Rob refused to swear against him that Argyll realises he does owe Rob and his family something, and gives Mary the cottage in the remote glen where she can hide.

However, Argyll does have a moral code over and above money, as he shows when says he will pay Rob's debts if Rob loses the duel. He is a relatively honourable man, but he is still part of the unfair system that cheats and discriminates against the Highlanders. Rob loses almost everything, and risks his life. Argyll fears and hates Montrose, but he will remain wealthy and secure as long as he protects himself.

Andrew Keir was one of Scotland's best-known and most senior actors, who trained at the Unity and Citizens Theatres and went on to appear in many television series in the sixties and seventies, Hammer Horror films and prestigious London stage plays such as *A Man for all Seasons* by Robert Bolt. *Rob Roy* was his last major film appearance. He died in 1997.

Alasdair Roy MacGregor

Alasdair Roy is Rob's younger brother. He is undisciplined and wild. He is quick to accuse MacDonald of treachery but fails to keep his own watch when it is essential. He is impetuous and thoughtless, constantly getting himself and others into trouble. He kills Killearn despite being told to protect him. His rash action in firing on the soldiers burning the township leads to Coll's death and his own.

Brian McCardie is from Glasgow. He began acting in amateur dramatics in Motherwell. On graduating from drama school his career focussed on stage and television roles, leading to appearances in shows such as *Taggart*, *Murder Most Horrid* and *River City*.

Coll
Coll is Rob's right-hand man, an older warrior who shares Rob's wisdom about tactics. He agrees with Rob (at the meeting of the Gregorach) that Montrose should not be attacked directly, and takes part in all Rob's adventures until the soldiers kill him. His death means Rob has lost one of his most trusted advisers.

Ewan Stewart has appeared in *Taggart*, *Rebus* and many other film and television productions.

Tam Sibbald
Tam Sibbald is the leader of the group of thieves whom Rob tracks at the start of the film, and whom he kills. Rob knew Tam when they were both young, kicking a football around with him at Crieff market. He and his band are 'broken men': people who have been cast out of their clans and live without protection. Rob knows that there are more and more like them in the Highlands, and that the clan system is breaking down.

David Hayman is one of Scotland's leading television, film and theatre actors, appearing in *A Sense of Freedom* (1979), *The Jackal* (1998) and *Ordinary Decent Criminal* (2000).

11. CRITICAL RECEPTION

Rob Roy opened to mixed reviews. Critics praised and condemned different aspects of the film, the only consensus being universal admiration for Tim Roth's performance. On almost every other part there was debate. Some saw confusion between the action and the romantic elements of the movie. Others felt that Liam Neeson's straightforwardly heroic role meant he was overshadowed by Roth, Hurt and Cox. Most were favourable towards Jessica Lange's performance. There was general acknowledgement that the swordfight scene was one of the best and most original in cinema. Other commentators felt that too much concern for historical detail distracted from the main story. *Braveheart*, released shortly after *Rob Roy*, and made mostly in Ireland, swiftly overhauled it at the box office and proved that year's blockbuster based in Scotland. However, *Rob Roy* was still a successful feature, playing in twenty-five major US cities on the first weekend of its release, reaching Number Two in the American box office in the first week of its release and Number One in the International box office in its first three weeks. It eventually earned $32 million in the US and about $65 million worldwide – a solid rather than a spectacular hit.[38]

It is easy to say that a film deserves more public attention than it receives. Of all the media, film especially depends on the paying audience and there is only one reaction to a new release that really matters: its box office receipts. But it is also true that *Rob Roy* brought to the big screen a unique collection of talents, Scottish-based, Scottish-born or from other countries, who produced an important film in a unique way. It contributed to the small but growing industry of Scottish film and portrayed one of Scotland's greatest legends in a way that was highly entertaining. It merged genres – the Scottish, the Western and the Hollywood costume drama or Heritage movie – in a manner that made a convincing and original contribution to the legend. It brought to Scottish film a concern for the authenticity of its national myths, and for the high quality of the finished product. Although not an outstanding box office success, it earned a considerable profit and gathered much critical praise. In the years since its release, it has continued to appeal to audiences and critics, and where films such as *Braveheart* are now seen as products of their time, *Rob Roy* has proved more timeless. Inspired by a legend, it updates and continues one of the most powerful traditions in Scottish story telling, the Romantic one, as well as successfully recasting its story in a contemporary mould. Taken as a whole, it remains the most convincing and entertaining big-budget historical film ever made or set in Scotland.

12. BIBLIOGRAPHY

General:

Aristotle, 'The Poetics', *Classical Literary Criticism* (Russell & Winterbottom, eds.), Oxford University Press: Oxford, 1989

Devine, Tom, *Scotland's Empire 1600-1815*, Penguin: London, 2004

Dick, Eddie, *From Limelight to Satellite*, BFI: London, 1991

Finney, Angus, *The State of European Cinema: A New Dose of Reality*, Cassell: London, 1996

Kitses, Jim and Rickman, Gregg (eds.), *The Western Reader*, First Limelight: New York, 1998

Lusted, David (ed.), *The Media Studies Book: A Guide for Teachers*, Routledge: London, 1991

McArthur (ed.), *Scotch Reels: Scotland in Cinema and Television*, bfi Publishing: London, 1982

Maltby, Richard, *Hollywood Cinema*, Blackwell: Oxford, 2003

Murray, W.H., *Rob Roy MacGregor: His Life and Times*, Canongate: Edinburgh, 1993

Murray, Jonathan 'Kids in America? Narratives of transatlantic influence in 1990s Scottish cinema', *Screen*, 2005

Petrie, Duncan, *Screening Scotland*, BFI: London, 2000

Riach, Alan, *Representing Scotland in Literature, Popular Culture and Iconography: The Masks of the Modern Nation*, Palgrave MacMillan: London, 2004

Scott, Sir Walter, *Rob Roy*, Penguin: London, 1995

Sillars, Jane and MacDonald, Myra, 'Gender, Spaces, Changes: Emergent Identities in a Scotland in Transition', in Neil Blain and David Hutchison (Eds.), *The Media in Scotland*, Edinburgh University Press: Edinburgh, 2008

Stevenson, David, *The Hunt for Rob Roy: The Man and the Myths*, Birlinn: Edinburgh, 2003

Thompson, Kristin, and Bordwell, David, *Film History: An Introduction*, McGraw Hill: London, 2003

Books about screenwriting:

Field, Syd, *Screenplay: The Foundations of Screenwriting*, Dell Publishing: New York, 1979

Goldman, William, *Adventures in the Screen Trade*, Abacus: New York, 1983

McKee, Robert, *Story*, Methuen: London, 1998

Vogler, Christopher, *The Hero's Journey*, Michael Wiese Productions: Studio City, 1992

Books and films by Alan Sharp:

Novels

A Green Tree in Gedde, New American Library: New York 1965

The Wind Shifts, Michael Joseph: London 1967

Films

The Hired Hand, directed by Peter Fonda, starring Peter Fonda, 1971

Ulzana's Raid, directed by Robert Aldritch, starring Burt Lancaster, 1972

Billy Two Hats, directed by Ted Kotcheff, starring Gregory Peck, 1974

Night Moves, directed by Arthur Penn, starring Gene Hackman, 1975

The Osterman Weekend, directed by Sam Peckinpah, starring Rutger Hauer, 1983

13. NOTES

1 Stevenson, p.286–287
2 Scott, p.408–409
3 Devine, p.122–123
4 W.H. Murray, p.54–55
5 Stevenson, p.268–285
6 Stevenson, p.xi. 'Murray's biography helped to inspire the 1995 Hollywood film *Rob Roy*, which contributed as much to historical understanding as Hollywood films usually do.'
7 Stevenson, p.190
8 Stevenson, p.186
9 Riach, p.82
10 W. H. Murray, p.130
11 Field, p.7
12 http://en.wikipedia.org/wiki/Alan_Sharp
13 Maltby, p.176
14 Finney, p.194
15 Finney, p.193–4
16 Finney, p.200
17 Thompson & Bordwell, p.415–6
18 Maltby, p.329
19 Aristotle, p.51
20 Sharp, *A Green Tree in Gedde*, p.77, '…they made the silk purse out of her sow's ear.' Rob uses the same expression with Mary at the Standing Stones.
21 Petrie, p.9
22 Lusted, p.123
23 Jonathan Murray, p.221
24 McArthur, p.17–39
25 McArthur, p.12–13
26 Sillars, p.186
27 McKee, p.197–197
28 Field, p.128
29 Maltby, p.75
30 Jonathan Murray, p.217–218
31 Petrie, p.53
32 Kitses & Rickman, p.389
33 W. H. Murray, p.51
34 Devine, p.128
35 Devine, p.120
36 Devine, p.129
37 Lusted, p.54–55
38 Finney, p.202

14. CAST LIST

Liam Neeson	...	Robert Roy MacGregor
Jessica Lange	...	Mary MacGregor
John Hurt	...	Montrose
Tim Roth	...	Archibald Cunningham
Eric Stoltz	...	Alan MacDonald
Andrew Keir	...	Duke of Argyll
Brian Cox	...	Killearn
Brian McCardie	...	Alasdair Roy MacGregor
Gilbert Martin	...	Will Guthrie
Vicki Masson	...	Betty
Gilly Gilchrist	...	Iain
Jason Flemyng	...	Gregor
Ewan Stewart	...	Coll
David Hayman	...	Tam Sibbald
Brian McArthur	...	Ranald MacGregor
David Brooks Palmer	...	Duncan MacGregor
Myra McFadyen	...	Tinker woman
Karen Matheson	...	Ceilidh singer
Shirley Henderson	...	Morag
John Murtagh	...	Referee
Bill Gardiner	...	Tavern lad
Valentine Nwanze	...	Servant boy
Richard Bonehill	...	Guthrie's opponent